P9-CBG-484

Practical Strategies for Cataloging Departments

Practical Strategies for Cataloging Departments

REBECCA L. LUBAS, EDITOR

ASBURY PARK PUBLIC LIBRARY
ASBURY PARK NEW JERSEY

Third Millennium Cataloging
SUSAN LAZINGER AND SHEILA INTNER, SERIES EDITORS

LIBRARIES UNLIMITED

AN IMPRINT OF ABC-CLIO, LLC
Santa Barbara, California • Denver, Colorado • Oxford, England

Copyright 2011 by Rebecca L. Lubas

All rights reserved. No part of this publication may be reproduced, stored in a retrieval system, or transmitted, in any form or by any means, electronic, mechanical, photocopying, recording, or otherwise, except for the inclusion of brief quotations in a review or reproducibles, which may be copied for classroom and educational programs only, without prior permission in writing from the publisher.

Library of Congress Cataloging-in-Publication Data

Practical strategies for cataloging departments / Rebecca L. Lubas, editor.
    p. cm. — (Third millennium cataloging)
Includes bibliographical references and index.
ISBN 978–1–59884–492–4 (alk. paper) — ISBN 978–1–59884–493–1 (ebook)
1. Cataloging. I. Lubas, Rebecca L.
Z693.P73   2010
025.3—dc22   2010040552

ISBN: 978–1–59884–492–4
EISBN: 978–1–59884–493–1

15 14 13 12 11   1 2 3 4 5

This book is also available on the World Wide Web as an eBook.
Visit www.abc-clio.com for details.

Libraries Unlimited
An Imprint of ABC-CLIO, LLC

ABC-CLIO, LLC
130 Cremona Drive, P.O. Box 1911
Santa Barbara, California 93116-1911

This book is printed on acid-free paper ∞

Manufactured in the United States of America

For the Cataloging and Discovery Services Department at the University of New Mexico Libraries. I'm lucky to work with this group of twenty-first-century catalogers!

Contents

Acknowledgments

As editor, I would like to thank all my colleagues who contributed to this volume for sharing their expertise so generously, as well as the series editors, Susan and Sheila, for their guiding wisdom and experienced eyes. I would also like to thank my University of New Mexico colleagues who have supported me with their advice, time, and understanding—especially my supervisor, Frances Wilkinson; my mentor, Johann van Reenen; and my dean, Martha Bedard. They have promoted the idea of "meeting users where they are" and helped me apply it to the world of cataloging.

I must acknowledge my colleagues, mentors, and friends from throughout my career—Sue Weiland, Amy Weiss, Carol Fleishauer, Sarah Mitchell, and the late, great Suzan Burks. Their wisdom is woven in this volume.

And, of course, I must thank my supportive spouse, Joseph McCarty!

Introduction: Managing the Challenge of the Twenty-First-Century Cataloging Department

Rebecca L. Lubas

The cataloging profession has undergone much upheaval in the course of the past 100 years: card distribution programs at the turn of the twentieth century, the first wide-scale machine-readable records in the mid-1960s, and faster, cheaper storage ushering in the integrated library system era in the 1970s and beyond. We have made use of new technology before the idea of the personal computer was a common one. Our profession rolled with these changes, adapted, and became more efficient.

And then came the Web.

The difference between this latest shift and the previous ones is the transformation of user behavior toward the library and, more so, of user behavior toward the world. We can no longer impose our standards on them. They demand from us. The information world as presented by search engines and social applications appears to bend to their demands, and they expect nothing less from us.

Of course, the golden age was never the present age. Even when we thought that we called the shots, we really did not. Users still failed to understand the difference between finding articles in one place and books in another. The best researchers were promoted to point that they never entered the library themselves but rather had graduate students toil over their searches for them.

Before the Web, users had little choice but to bend to the will of our approved controlled vocabularies, and they reluctantly learned to speak our language. However, the Web has raised the stakes. We cannot simply answer that instant turnaround of metadata is not possible, so the user must wait for discovery and access. Users would not believe us. We have to make it possible. We have to meet users where they are, when they are.

Ideas in this essay originally presented in a paper at the ISTEC *V International Symposium on Digital Libraries*, October 27, 2009 in Albuquerque, NM.

In the digital library, catalogers (or metadata creators) can no longer remain behind the desk in isolation. The cataloging profession has a long tradition of organizing and analyzing information using internationally recognized standards. In the digital library world, there are many more standards, many more information consumers, and much more information than before. In order to respond to today's information needs, metadata creators need to multiply both their skill set and their interactions with consumers of information.

How do we do this? We build on the blocks that made cataloging operations successful models of cooperative work for a century. We have to think bigger and build worldwide communities of practice. The foundation for an expanded metadata creation community is solid, refined for at least a century and practiced in improving and interpreting a standard. We will need to expand and improve flexibility to incorporate more standards and more points of view. Expansion can be achieved by complementing the formal organizations of our profession to constantly forge new information connections (Kimble 2008, 463). We need to look within the cataloging community for new approaches and interpretations in our practices, evaluating their usefulness and testing our assumptions. We will also need to expand our community beyond career catalogers to users of metadata standards other than the *Anglo-American Cataloguing Rules* and the MARC encoding format. We also need to engage end users. Since communities that share values develop a common worldview, by expanding our community, we will expand our view (Hislop 2004, 38). Managers of cataloging departments face many challenges that can be met by sharing best practices, an approach that has served us well and is now even more of a necessity.

In this volume, we look at the challenges and opportunities of the twenty-first-century catalog manager. We examine the issues with implementing a major update to our cornerstone professional standard with the transition from the *Anglo-American Cataloguing Rules* to *Resource Description and Access*. This change comes at a time when our guiding light for interpretation of standards, the Library of Congress, is changing its role. This is a major shift for cataloging, and we discuss how catalog managers change their practices to progress as these changes come.

As our profession is moving toward one of multiple standards, we will delve into the issues presented by transitioning from a single standard profession to a polyglot one. Training a twenty-first-century cataloger is a different task than training yesterday's cataloger, and we look at strategies to develop current catalogers and new ones. Economic necessity and wise use of labor demand that we consider outsourcing and vendor cataloging products as options to maximize our efforts and resources. We may also have our own products to offer—both in remixing our MARC data into useful discovery tools and in consulting using our well-honed expertise in new situations.

Catalogers have opportunities to interact with their library peers in other departments in ways that did not exist previously, as libraries implement new discovery tools and venture into new information platforms and data repositories. We discuss how to approach new and refreshed collaboration with other library departments. As libraries need to be creative in seeking resources, we also look at strategies for participating in grant funding with our colleagues.

Cataloging has the potential to become a vibrant twenty-first-century profession. We hope this volume can help you get started making your contribution to making that potential a reality.

REFERENCES

Hislop, D. (2004). The paradox of communities of practice. In P. Hildreth & C. Kimble (Eds.), 36–44. *Knowledge Networks: Innovation through Communities of Practice*. Hershey, PA: IGI Global.

Kimble, C. (2008). Some success factors for the communal management of knowledge. *International Journal of Information Management, 28* (6), 461–67.

CHAPTER 1

Evolving Standards: Making the Jump to RDA in Historical Context

Robert L. Bothmann

Lubetzky's *Code of Cataloging Rules*
Cutter's *Rules for a Dictionary Catalog*
Ranganathan's *The Five Laws of Library Science*

We hear them, we know them, we read them in library school, but do we really understand them? "They" include not only the groundbreaking models, codes, and standards listed above but also all standards we use in the discipline of library and information science. Standards are the lifeblood of the information science profession. Without standards to govern our creation, dissemination, and presentation of surrogate records in a catalog, users would have no reliable means of locating information and understanding the information they retrieve in any kind of search. Standards enable libraries to achieve their goals through the sharing of resources and consistency of access (Harris 2001, 526; McCallum 1996, 5–6). In the library sphere, standards have not been a static creation that blossomed fully formed; rather, they have formed through a (r)evolutionary process, adapting to a changing information environment and simultaneously causing upheaval in the cataloging profession.

The standards that structure the niche in the library information sphere known as cataloging are based on principles articulated by Anthony Panizzi, Charles Coffin Jewett, Charles A. Cutter, S. R. Ranganathan, and Seymour Lubetzky, about which every first-year information science student learns. Collectively, the intellectual work of these men form the core of cataloging theory and influence the way catalogers construct and amend existing standards. These principles, although developed by generations past primarily for printed materials collocated in a linear, analog card or book catalog, still serve us in our contemporary age dominated by nonprint materials described in machine-readable form in a nonlinear, digital space. Lynne C. Howarth (1998) first proposed the idea of the genealogy of the cataloging code, offering the characterization that the Anglo-American cataloging rules enjoy a pedigree "from a line of bibliographic ancestors, reflecting influences" based on the genetic makeup, or theory and seminal works, from Panizzi to the International Federation of Library Associations and Institutions (IFLA) (15).

By extension of the genealogical metaphor, the genetic makeup of biological organisms (or cataloging theory) changes over time in succeeding generations, ultimately producing a new species (or cataloging codes) through the process of evolution, which in our compressed human time spans seems more like a revolution for each occurrence. The jump from the *Anglo-American Cataloguing Rules*, 2nd edition (AACR2) (American Library Association [ALA] 1978) to its (r)evolution into *RDA: Resource Description & Access* (RDA) begins by looking back at the genealogy of the cataloging rules.

THE FOSSIL RECORD (OR HISTORICAL REVIEW)

Very little discussion of cataloging standards appears in LISA or LISTA™ in the period between 1960 and 1970 pertaining to the predominant rules in use in the at that time—namely, the Library of Congress (1949) *Rules for Descriptive Cataloging in the Library of Congress* and the ALA's *A.L.A. Cataloging Rules for Author and Title Entries*, each published and used between 1949 and 1967. Many of the issues facing catalogers and code revision during the early twentieth century were addressed by Wyllis Wright (1976) in "The Anglo-American Cataloging Rules: A Historical Perspective." Knowlton (2009) reviews the debates over cataloging code reform leading up to the *Anglo-American Cataloging Rules* (AACR) in *Library Resources & Technical Services* in the 1960s, which, as the author notes, was primarily a medium for news and debate and not the scholarly venue it is today (17). After the publication and implementation of AACR (ALA 1967), however, the literature begins to show a number of critiques ranging from detailed analyses of specific rules (Guha and Rajan 1967a, 1967b) and comments on perceived defects (Gilbert 1967; Hamdy 1973). Kelm (1978) offers the context presented in Wright (1976) as the basis for calling the revision of AACR "as evolutionary rather than revolutionary" (22). More often, the literature shows commentary on the shortcomings of AACR in respect to nonprint resources (Hagler 1975; Library Association 1973; Merrett and Sedgley 1974; Quinly 1972; Schrader 1974), which were arguably the primary motivation for the revisions that resulted in AACR2, first published in 1978 (Chan 2007, 58).

While the 1978 manifestation of AACR2 dealt well with the nonprint formats of the era and subsequent revisions and updates (ALA 1988, 1998, 2002) addressed changes reflecting the technology of the time and loosened restrictions on rules allowing for more adaptability with new and emerging technologies, the literature of the cataloging profession focused more on automation and globalization between 1990 and 2000 than it did on cataloging codes and standards. Since the 1980s and 1990s were also an era of cataloger retrenchment (Leyson and Boydston 2005; Steinhagen, Hanson, and Moynahan 2007; Wilder 2002), outsourced cataloging (Dunkle 1996), consolidation of cataloging departments (Leysen and Boydston 2005), and the creation of technical services departments from the merger of cataloging, acquisitions, and serials departments (Anderson 2008; Branton and Englert 2002; Coats and Kiegel 2003), we can see that catalogers had other issues on their minds. In fact, the literature at the end of the twentieth century shows a primary focus on the perceptions of education and training of catalogers (Carter 1987; Hill 2002) and reflections on the future of cataloging (Connell and Maxwell 2000; Schottlaender 1998; Weihs 1998).

With the publication of the *Rules for Descriptive Cataloging in the Library of Congress* in 1949, we see the early development of efforts to review and revise, beginning with Lubetzky's work in 1951 and the adoption in 1961 of the Statement of Principles, better known as the "Paris Principles" (IFLA 1961), culminating in the 1967 publication of AACR. By 1974, the cataloging community had a deep desire to reform AACR, substantiated by the formation of a new international body called the Joint Steering Committee *for the Revision of AACR* (emphasis added), commonly referred to as the JSC. The JSC (comprised of representatives from ALA, the British Library, the Canadian Committee on Cataloguing [representing the Association pour l'avancement des sciences et des techniques de la documentation, the Canadian Library Association, and Libraries and Archives Canada], the Library Association [United Kingdom], the Library of Congress, and, since 1981, the Australian Committee on Cataloguing) prepared the second edition of AACR in 1978 and AACR2's three subsequent revisions (Joint Steering Committee for Development of RDA 2009; Libraries and Archives Canada 2009). By 1998, more serious thought was given to a bigger evolutionary step—AACR3, which was often discussed in some of the future-of-cataloging symposia held in the 1990s (Connell and Maxwell 2000; Schottlaender 1998; Weihs 1998). Maxwell (2000), for example, muses on a few concepts of desired AACR2 evolution in an essay based on reactions to the Lubetzky Symposium held at the University of California, Los Angeles, in 1998. She ends her essay with a premonitory question, asking if new rules ought to build on Lubetzky's concepts of work distinguished from editions, translations, and versions. Maxwell (2000, 160) then suggested Martha Yee's (1998) "What Is a Work?," which itself is, along with Yee's and Barbara Tillett's doctoral dissertations under Elaine Svenonius, a prelude to the *Functional Requirements for Bibliographic Records* (FRBR) (IFLA 2009a) conceptual model (Martha Yee, personal communication).

The cataloging literature at the turn of the century abruptly changes focus from cataloging standards' future to concentrating primarily on "metadata" in a general sense, typically in relation to Dublin Core and other schemas (El-Sherbini 2001; El-Sherbini and Klim 2004; Guenther 2003; LeVan 2001). This attention to the concept of metadata, above and beyond that created using AACR2 encoded in MARC format, can arguably be the result of the profession's lack of attention to or action on cataloging code revision during the preceding decade, the attrition of professionals, the more blended duties of catalogers unrelated to cataloging specifically, and the dawning realization that the Internet and its associated technologies created formats not easily described in a user-centered manner by conventional standards. In other words, a declining population of professionals who had little time to devote to cataloging and whose interest was focused mainly on cataloging education, metadata, and hope for a new cataloging code to address electronic resources were so distracted by these topics that the advent of the twenty-first century and its associated access and presentation media blew by them beyond almost any hope or ability to rewrite AACR2 to catch up.

Indeed, we see a sudden flurry of activity to rewrite AACR2 chapters 3 (maps), 9 (computer files), and 12 (serials) for late twentieth-century needs, which were quickly integrated into a 2002 AACR2 revision, renaming the afore mentioned chapters as cartographic materials, electronic resources, and continuing and integrating resources, respectively. Thereafter, the JSC issued only three minor updates. Cataloging code revision effectively ended with the 2002 revision and has been essentially stalled for the better part of the past decade. Lest we lose all hope for change, the JSC gave a nod toward the cataloging code (r)evolution by changing its name to the Joint Steering Committee *for Development of RDA* (emphasis added).

These changes we see in cataloging literature are manifested in the features and relationships to other standards that are part of the basis for the realization of RDA (ALA 2008, 0.1, 0.2). One might ask if this is the evolutionary change that Maxwell (2000, 159) and Gorman and Oddy (1998, 158) argue for, or if it is the revolutionary change that Gorman opposes (Gorman 1998; 2007, 60; Gorman and Oddy 1998, 158).

PRINCIPLES

Gorman and Oddy (1998) outline Lubetzky's imprint on AACR2, noting that many of the "features of AACR2 were . . . compromises based on political and practical exigencies" (159), which they feel can be excised without harm to the Paris Principles on which it is based. Both Maxwell (2000, 160) and Gorman and Oddy (1998, 159) are quick to point out the importance of the 1961 Paris Principles and their integral relationship with AACR2, which followed six years after the adoption of the principles by the International Conference on Cataloguing Principles. We see in this a reiteration of what has come before: IFLA recently revised and adopted a new "Paris Principles" ahead of the release of RDA—the Statement of International Cataloguing Principles (IFLA 2009b; see also Creider 2009).

Gorman and Oddy (1998) summarize the principles on which AACR2 is based as descriptions formulated according to the *International Standard Bibliographic Description* (ISBD) (IFLA 2007) and based on the item, the equal treatment of all media, and the derivation of access points based on the nature of the work, all of which stem from the Paris Principles (Gorman and Oddy 1998, 159) and are strikingly similar to many of the principles of RDA.

RDA's principles are based on FRBR and the *Functional Requirements for Authority Data* (FRAD) (Joint Steering Committee for Development of RDA 2010, 10.1) both of which influenced the revision of the Paris Principles into the Statement of International Cataloguing Principles (Creider 2009, 592–93; Joint Steering Committee for Development of RDA 2010, 3.2). To summarize, the principles of RDA are to find, identify, select, obtain, and understand (ALA 2008, 0.4.2.1) and moreover to provide relationships between multiple entities from other resources, authors, and publishers to works, editions, and corporate bodies (Chapman 2008, 29). RDA descriptions are still based on the item (ALA 2008, 0.4.3.4) and still compatible with ISBD (ALA, 2008, 0.2). The equal treatment of media is immediately expressed in RDA (ALA 2008, 0.0), which is further supported by IFLA's Statement of International Cataloguing Principles' active inclusion of all media, in stark contrast to the Paris Principles' (and, by association, AACR2's) bibliocentric perspective (Creider 2009, 584–85).

IMPLEMENTATION OF AACR2

Contrary to Kelm (1978), Gorman and Oddy (1998, 158) state that AACR2 was a "radical departure" from AACR, which was opposed by many catalogers and administrators, in what is now called the "War of AACR2" (Berry 1980; Gorman 2007, 69–70; Martell 1981, 4). The "War of AACR2" included some critical commentary from Lubetzky (2001), who said that AACR2 is "inconsistent with the traditions of Anglo-American cataloging." The changes in the second edition were so profound that many libraries expected to close their card catalogs and start new ones for AACR2 descriptions, to which Lubetzky is said to have uttered, "We're not closing catalogs, we're dismembering them" (Berry 1980, 1243).

The "price" of AACR2 implementation was too high for many, which Berry (1980) attributes as having a "great potential for alienating users, creating catalog chaos, and forcing huge expense" (1243). While some opposition questioned the "price" in terms of principles, it was clear that the "price" of AACR2 implementation was more about cost than anything fundamentally flawed about the code and that opposition came largely from library directors who suddenly began to pay attention to the transition to AACR2.

The literature on the "War of AACR2" consistently mentions the outrage of library directors. Even though they are people paid to worry about budgets, the timbre of these articles suggests that there was slightly more concern for the experience of the user, particularly from Martell (1981), than the budgetary expenses any plans of change would impose. Now, three decades later, we do not see much of any public concern from directors regarding RDA. This is invariably due to the fact that we do not rely on analog card catalogs anymore, so any expense in RDA implementation is likely to be absorbed in integrated library systems work and not as easily quantifiable as it was for the implementation of AACR2 (Hopkins and Edens 1986; Pang 1980).

In fact, the general sentiment appears to be that AACR2 was a better, more logical code (R.M.D. 1980), but the "radical" change was in the construction and form of headings. Most of the objections to the new, "radical" headings rested in the belief that users would have difficulty finding materials (Berry 1980; Martin 1980; R.M.D. 1980), but it seems difficult to accept (perhaps as one whose entire professional career has dealt only with AACR2) that "Minnesota. University." makes more logical sense to a user than "University of Minnesota."

This (r)evolutionary change in the construction of access points and the associated costs in retrospective conversion of existing headings caused the directors of the Association of Research Libraries' member libraries to force the Library of Congress to delay implementation of AACR2 for two years (until 1981). This in turn forced the Library of Congress to delay ending their practice known as superimposition, a policy whereby the Library of Congress used AACR rules to create new headings but continued to use headings already established under ALA (1949) rules (Maxwell 2004, xvi; Taylor and Paff 1986, 272). This meant that large runs of cards did not need to be changed right away but also forced libraries to wait for Library of Congress catalog cards to appear before they could know what form had been used. The delay in implementation of AACR2 then created even more records that would need to be changed later under de-superimposition, adding to the eventual expense (Hopkins and Edens 1986, 7).

The Association of College and Research Libraries found in a survey that very few libraries had planned for any change and were waiting until the consequences of the switch were clear (American Library Association, Resources and Technical Services Division 1980). Some libraries began interfiling cards in their card catalogs rather than waiting, and others closed their catalogs with AACR descriptions and began new ones for AACR2 (R.M.D. 1980). Pang (1980, 208–9) presented a plan for interfiling at a medium-sized library that estimated that 707 personnel hours were needed to correct existing headings and bring them into compliance with AACR2. Another example can be seen in Texas A&M's (1981) decision to research the most likely heading changes, make new cards, and exchange them in the catalog over two and a half days. At least one library, the University of Illinois at Urbana-Champaign, opted to begin using AACR2 on the original schedule of January 1980, which meant that original cataloging had to be withheld from national bibliographic utilities until the official 1981 implementation (University of Illinois 1980).

AACR2 TRANSITION TO RDA

Interestingly, Gorman and Oddy (1998) suggest that the naming convention of "second edition" for AACR2 may be an underlying cause for our current crisis of faith regarding the need for revision in the cataloging community:

It is also entirely possible that such a new name would have meant . . . that regular revisions of the code could have taken place in an orderly, nondisputatious manner freed from the idea that change means a new code, an "AACR3." (158)

In other words, Gorman and Oddy (1998, 158–59) are saying that AACR2 by any other name would have allowed for constant evolution rather than the stop-and-go situation we are entering now, in which we end AACR2 and move to RDA. That change and evolution in the standard requires wholesale change of name and identity (like a new species) is evidenced by the aborted attempt to move to AACR3, which failed because of its perpetuation of carrier-based rule arrangements and library jargon-filled rules, among other things (Joint Steering Committee for Development of RDA 2005). Yet, as it stands, RDA is simply AACR2 repackaged, leaner, meaner, and ill fitting over a brand-new theoretical skeleton (FRBR), as yet untested in its ability to bear the weight of the bibliographic universe (Chapman 2008; Coyle 2008; Coyle and Hillman 2007).

In a sense, the evolution of AACR2 to RDA is the inverse of the evolution of the U.S. MARC format integration. Format integration required the US MARC formats for each material type to be combined into one work form. While variable data fields were fully integrated, variable control fields were not (in order to accommodate legacy data in existing records), which has resulted in the hybrid, almost-integrated MARC 21 format we have today (Highsmith 1993, 2–6). Where format integration creates one view of out of many, RDA, through its implementation of FRBR, creates many "records" or "views" (one for each entity) out of one catalog record. That is, with AACR2, catalogers make one record that describes the work, expression, and manifestation—sometimes even the item. These elements are discernible to the trained human eye but not easily parsed by the user, the novice cataloger, or the computer. FRBR and RDA allow, in theory, for each entity to be split out into discrete records.

Another feature of (r)evolution in the cataloging code can be seen in the manner of use in which the cataloger accesses the rules. AACR2 was written to be used in a linear manner, beginning with part 1, Description, and chapter 1, General Rules, transcribing information in linear order from eight numbered areas of description. The rules within each area are ordered and subordered to match the order in which these data elements are to be displayed on the catalog card and, by extension, in the MARC record. The cataloger then proceeds to the carrier-specific chapter in part 1 and complies with any specific instructions for the format for each area. Thereafter, the cataloger must move to part 2, where she follows detailed rules to choose the main entry (yet another analog, card-based activity) and select all other access points. After that selection is completed, the cataloger must then follow multiple rules to create the form of the name or title entries required based on the access point selections. This process must be repeated for each and every discrete bibliographic entity requiring a surrogate record. In practice, AACR2 cataloging is not quite this onerous because we can derive descriptions from similar, related surrogate records and much of the work involved with recording headings has already been established and made available in the authority file. AACR2 is then decidedly a linear, analog-based system of rules printed on paper in a bound (and later, wisely, a loose-leaf) book[1] that prescribes descriptive order and display—everything that RDA purports not to be (Joint Steering Committee for Development of RDA 2010).

Rather than a book, the JSC intends RDA to be published in an online-only format (Joint Steering Committee for Development of RDA 2010, 7.2), thus placing the code in a digital space that has no relative order; that is, there is no "begin here" and "end here." The cataloger creates the "analog" or ordered path, also called a work flow, for any particular type of resource. As mentioned before, RDA is compatible with ISBD, but RDA does not prescribe ISBD display or any other display for that matter (Joint Steering Committee for Development of RDA 2010, 4.5). Rather than descriptive areas based on ISBD, RDA allows the cataloger to record the attributes of the various FRBR entities (manifestation, item, work, expression, names, concepts, objects, events, and places) and then to record the relationships amongst those and other related entities (ALA 2008, 0.5). In theory, each entity type would have its own record, and the cataloger simply links various records together with different types of defined relationships, such as the relationship of the author to the work or the relationship of the publisher to the manifestation. In practice, the cataloger will use the same flat MARC 21 bibliographic record structure.

MAKING THE LEAP

The evolution of cataloging codes and their usage in cataloging has had a decided impact on the work flow, indeed even the terminology that we practice and use daily. In the days of the card catalog, one could probably discuss cataloging purely in terms of ISBD areas of description. This, however, does require the use of specific words, such as "parallel title in area 1 title information." After decades of encoding AACR2 descriptions in MARC format, you may find it difficult to express cataloging ideas in ISBD area-related descriptive terms—in fact, you may even be met with blank stares since many catalogers seem not to know the AACR2/ISBD description areas. Expressing a data element as "245 subfield b" may lead to instant recognition by many catalogers. Ultimately, this identification is imprecise, as the 245 $b is used to encode the area 1 parallel title as well as area 1 other title information (not limited to but often referred to as the subtitle), and both elements may in fact also be recorded in the 245 $c under certain circumstances.

The point here is that many of us have allowed our understanding and use of AACR2 to be dictated and interpreted by the MARC format when in fact it should be the other way around. Thus, one of the first tasks that any cataloger must accomplish to make the leap to RDA is to disassociate all MARC conventions, presentation elements, and prescriptions for punctuation with AACR2, which may be easier said than done. Those who have a solid understanding of cataloging in terms of AACR2's areas of description will likely have a much easier time transitioning to RDA and selecting appropriate MARC codes for encoding specific data elements outlined in RDA rules.

It is one thing to sit down every day and describe materials, add some access points, slap a few subjects on the record, and call it "cataloged." A lot of thinking, evaluation, trial and error, theory, and common sense have gone into that which we so freely practice on a daily basis. Many of us do so without thinking about it, much the same way our cars drive themselves to work along familiar routes every day, our being mere passengers behind the wheel.

One day, however, something changes on your way to work, such as a new job necessitating a new route to the workplace or road construction that causes a detour. The standard has changed, and you must learn it and adapt to it, whether by following the GPS voice, looking at that Google™ map you printed, or watching for department of transportation road signs directing you along an alternate route. You still know how to drive the car (how to catalog), you just have to learn the route (RDA rules) to get you to your destination (the catalog record).

Lubetzky, Cutter, and Ranganathan, among others, provide overarching philosophies for cataloging (driving), similar to the way your high school driver's education course did. You have been driving for years, and you know how to do it, so learning the new route to the workplace or getting used to driving a fancy new car is made easier because you already know the principles behind the driving.

RDA is no different. The principles have not changed, only the controls. Margaret Maxwell (2000, 158–59) described this sentiment of following the new rules without fully understanding the principles right away. For her, the epiphany came at a monthlong seminar in 1967 on the principles and theory imbued in AACR led by Lubetzky at the University of Illinois at Urbana-Champaign. The transition from AACR2 to RDA is not new territory. We have been there before, stalled it, disparaged it, retired because of it, and still succeeded at transitioning in spite of it. We are moving from a circular steering wheel to a high-end joystick that senses our intended moves before we make them. The roadway is still made of asphalt or concrete, you still drive on the correct side of the road (right or left; depending on your Anglo-location, it is the correct side!), and there is still a centerline stripe and a speed limit. Our advantage as catalogers over drivers is, however, that there are no cataloging police!

Since RDA is built on the FRBR data model of work, expression, manifestation, and item, the other major leap that catalogers will need to make is the idea of distinguishing these four concepts with different types of description records. RDA in essence relies on linkages of a work record to an expression record to a manifestation record to an item record (not to be confused with the item record in an integrated library system that bears the barcode and is used for circulation purposes), each of which may be linked to entity records and potentially to other work and expression records. This data model assumes that a relational database structure exists that can accommodate these linkages and display the relationships to catalogers and users alike.

A database such as this does not exist, but in the ideal RDA universe, the cataloger who needs to create a fully original record would need to create the following:

- A work record
- An expression record
- A manifestation record
- An item record
- All entity 2 name records
- All entity 3 records (concepts, objects, events, and places)
- All related entity 1 records (related work, expression, manifestation, and item)

Once created, these records must then be linked. In a more typical work flow, most catalogers would need to create only the entity 1 records required for the resource and link to the other entity records.

Until that fictional database becomes nonfiction, most of us will record the data elements required for entity 1 records in a flat MARC file. The closest we will get to relational linkages will be the access point references we use for subjects, names, and titles that may or may not have an authority record. The authority record is analogous to an entity 2 record, for example. Adding to this is the complication noted by Mayernik's (2010) study on MARC field distribution, which shows a strict adherence of MARC tags that are directly related to AACR2 areas of description and access points but minimal use of the 76X-78X linking entry MARC tags, most of which have no concrete AACR2 rule equivalent. Mayernik (2010, 48–49) posits that a more liberal use of the linking entry fields could make our existing AACR2 MARC records and, by extension, our coming RDA MARC records more FRBR and RDA friendly.

CONCLUSION

RDA has been focus of a wide range of remarks and critiques, ranging from Gorman's solid stance against the need for a new code (Gorman 1998; 2007, 60; Gorman and Oddy 1998, 158) to Coyle's (2008) and Coyle and Hillman's

(2007) discerning assessment of RDA's somewhat backward, text-based communication. The professional community has long had concerns about the viability of the standard (Bowen 2006, 4–5), some of which have manifested as clever witticisms, such as Robert Ellett's "I hope it doesn't end like a book on the Titanic (that is, sunk before you can finish reading it)" (personal communication).

Hopkins and Edens (1986) noted that various communication tools, like the *Alternative Cataloging Newsletter* (published in microfiche) and a column in the ALA Resources and Technical Services' *RTSD Newsletter*, were created expressly for the implementation of AACR2 and abruptly ceased in December 1980. The ALA Resources and Technical Services Division (now known as the Association for Library Collections & Technical Services) Cataloging and Classification Section's Catalog Maintenance Discussion Group held a program called "AACR2 Six Months After: Are Things Going as Planned?" at the 1981 ALA annual conference to review the implementation, and little discussion ever followed (Hopkins and Edens 1986, 10, 12). We see a similar parallel in this transition time, except, instead of provocatively publishing in microfiche, we see countless blog entries and discussion list posts and have held several preconferences and workshops at various venues all devoted to RDA preparation. If we hold true to our history, most of our profession's discussions about RDA implementation will abruptly fade away, like a mass-extinction event, somewhere around June 2012.

When we consider that evolution is the adaptation or response to a change in the environment to take advantage of new opportunities, it follows that the code (RDA) ought to be a response to the database environment (e.g., MARC 21, the catalog). However, RDA may be less of a gradual evolution based on natural selection to adapt and take advantage of a changed environment than it is an X-Men–like mutation that creates a changed entity that is evolved beyond the ability of the environment to support it. It is certainly a code with a mutation that must grapple and suffer under the limitations of the un-evolved database environment in which it is being birthed. Although we can use the rules of RDA now and create accurate descriptions, catalogers in the library sphere are limited by existing schema, such as MARC 21, and environments, such as commercial integrated library systems built for MARC records. RDA requires a relational database ocean in which to thrive and prosper. But the current environment may make RDA more like a mudpuppy— able to live in water and on land but not so agile out of the water. The real test will come when we want to implement a relational database and disassemble the flat MARC records to create a true FRBR, FRAD, and RDA structure.

NOTE

1. AACR2 is also available in HTML form in *Cataloger's Desktop*, in which form it provides the ability to link to referenced rules, glossary entries,

Library of Congress rule interpretations, MARC tags, and other, related rules. However, the intended reading order and use of AACR2 in this form remain linear.

BIBLIOGRAPHY

American Library Association. *A.L.A. Cataloging Rules for Author and Title Entries*. Chicago: American Library Association, 1949.

American Library Association. *Anglo-American Cataloging Rules*. North American text. Chicago: American Library Association, 1967.

American Library Association. *Anglo-American Cataloguing Rules*. 2nd ed. Chicago: American Library Association, 1978.

American Library Association. *Anglo-American Cataloguing Rules*. 2nd ed., 1988 rev. Chicago: American Library Association, 1988.

American Library Association. *Anglo-American Cataloguing Rules*. 2nd ed., 2002 rev. Chicago: American Library Association, 2002.

American Library Association. *RDA: Resource Description & Access*. (Constituency review draft.) Chicago: American Library Association, 2008. Available at http://www.rdaonline.org/constituencyreview

American Library Association, Resources and Technical Services Division. "RTSD Cataloging Committee to Handle 'AACR 2' Queries." *Library Journal* 105, no. 4 (April 1980): 899–900.

Anderson, Rick. "Future-Proofing the Library: Strategies for Acquisitions, Cataloging, and Collection Development." *Serials Librarian* 55, no. 4 (November 2008): 560–67.

Berry, John. " 'AACR 2'—A Prudent Postponement." *Library Journal* 105, no. 11 (June 1980): 1243.

Bowen, Jennifer. "RDA: Resource Description and Access Part A, Chapters 6–7. Constituency Review of June 2006 Draft." September 25, 2006. http://www.rda-jsc.org/docs/5rda-parta-ch6&7-alaresp.pdf (accessed March 15, 2010).

Branton, Ann, and Tracy Englert. "Mandate for Change: Merging Acquisitions and Cataloging Functions into a Single Workflow." *Library Collections, Acquisitions, & Technical Services* 26, no. 4 (Winter 2002): 345–54.

Carter, Ruth C., ed. *Education and Training for Catalogers and Classifiers. Cataloging & Classification Quarterly*, vol. 7, no. 4. New York: Haworth Press, 1987.

Chan, Lois Mai. *Cataloging and Classification: An Introduction*. 3rd ed. Lanham, MD: Scarecrow Press, 2007.

Chapman, Ann. "RDA: A Cataloging Code for the 21st Century." *Library + Information Update* 7, no. 9 (September 2008): 28–30.

Coats, Jacqueline, and Joseph Kiegel. "Automating the Nexus of Book Selection, Acquisitions and Rapid Copy Cataloging." *Library Collections, Acquisitions, & Technical Services* 27, no. 1 (2003): 33–44.

Connell, Tschera Harkness, and Robert L. Maxwell, eds. *The Future of Cataloging: Insights from the Lubetzky Symposium: April 18, 1998,*

University of California, Los Angeles. Chicago: American Library Association, 2000.

Coyle, Karen. "R&D: RDA in RDF, or: Can Resource Description Become Rigorous Data?" (annotated version of presentation). Code4Lib2008, March 2008. http://www.slideshare.net/eby/karen-coyle-keynote-rd -can-resource-description-become-rigorous-data (accessed March 15, 2010).

Coyle, Karen, and Diane Hillman. "Resource Description and Access (RDA): Cataloging Rules for the 20th Century." *D-Lib Magazine* 13, no. 1–2 (January/February 2007). http://www.dlib.org/dlib/january07/coyle/01 coyle.html (accessed March 15, 2010).

Creider, Laurence S. "A Comparison of the Paris Principles and the International Cataloguing Principles." *Cataloging & Classification Quarterly* 47, no. 6 (2009): 583–99.

Cutter, Charles A. *Rules for a Dictionary Catalogue*. 2nd ed. Special Report on Public Libraries, Part II. Washington, DC: Government Printing Office, 1889.

Dunkle, Clare B. "Outsourcing the Catalog Department: A Meditation Inspired by the Business and Library Literature." *Journal of Academic Librarianship* 22, no. 1 (January 1996): 33.

El-Sherbini, Magda. "Metadata and the Future of Cataloging." *Library Review* 50, no. 1/2 (2001): 16–27.

El-Sherbini, Magda, and George Klim. "Metadata and Cataloging Practices." *Electronic Library* 22, no. 3 (July 2004): 238–48.

Gilbert, John. 1967. *New Code, Old Problems: A Critical Discussion of Some Aspects of the Anglo-American Cataloguing Rules (1967)*. North East London Polytechnic Library Occasional Paper, no. 1. London: North East London Polytechnic Library, 1971.

Gorman, Michael. "AACR3? Not!" In *The Future of the Descriptive Cataloging Rules*, ed. Brian E. C. Schottlaender, 19–29. Chicago: American Library Association, 1998.

Gorman, Michael. "The True History of AACR2, 1968–1988: A Personal Memoir by One Who Was There." In *Commemorating the Past, Celebrating the Present, Creating the Future*, ed. Pamela Bluh, 60–74. Chicago: American Library Association, 2007.

Gorman, Michael, and Pat Oddy. "The Anglo-American Cataloguing Rules, Second Edition: Their History and Principles." In *The Principles and Future of AACR*, ed. Jean R. Weihs, 158–65. Ottawa: Canadian Library Association, 1998.

Guenther, Rebecca S. "MODS: The Metadata Object Description Schema." *portal: Libraries & the Academy* 3, no. 1 (January 2003): 137–50.

Guha, B., and T. N. Rajan. "The Anglo-American Cataloging Rules, with Emphasis on Rule 3 (Works on Shared Authorship)." *Annals of Library Science & Documentation* 14, no. 3 (1967a): 143–51.

Guha, B., and T. N. Rajan. "The Anglo-American Cataloging Rules with Emphasis on Rule 6 (Serials)." *Annals of Library Science & Documentation* 14, no. 4 (1967b): 206–11.

Hagler, Ronald. "The Development of Cataloging Rules for Nonbook Materials." *Library Resources & Technical Services* 19, no. 3 (1975): 268–78.

Hamdy, M. Nabil. *The Concept of Main Entry as Represented in the Anglo-American Cataloging Rules: A Critical Appraisal with Some Suggestions: Author Main Entry vs. Title Main Entry.* Research Studies in Library Science, no. 10. Littleton, CO: Libraries Unlimited, 1973.

Harris, Patricia R. "Why Standards Matter." *portal: Libraries and the Academy* 1, no. 4 (2001): 525–29.

Highsmith, Anne L. "Format Integration: An Overview." In *Format Integration and Its Effect on Cataloging, Training, and Systems,* ed. Karen Coyle, 1–10. Chicago: American Library Association, 1993.

Hill, Janet Swan, ed. *Education for Cataloging and the Organization of Information: Pitfalls and the Pendulum.* Binghamton, NY: Haworth Information Press, 2002.

Hopkins, Judith, and John A. Edens, eds. *Research Libraries and Their Implementation of AACR2.* Foundations in Library and Information Science, vol. 22. Greenwich, CT: JAI Press, 1986.

Howarth, Lynne C. "Key Lessons of History: Revisiting the Foundations of AACR." In *The Future of the Descriptive Cataloging Rules,* ed. Brian E. C. Schottlaender, 6–18. Chicago: American Library Association, 1998.

International Federation of Library Associations and Institutions. *Functional Requirements for Bibliographic Records* (amended and corrected). The Hague: International Federation of Library Associations and Institutions, 2009a. http://www.ifla.org/en/publications/functional-requirements-for-bibliographic -records (accessed March 15, 2010).

International Federation of Library Associations and Institutions. *International Standard Bibliographic Description.* Preliminary consolidated ed. IFLA Series on Bibliographic Control, vol. 31. Munich: K. G. Saur, 2007. http://www .ifla.org/en/publications/international-standard-bibliographic-description (accessed March 15, 2010).

International Federation of Library Associations and Institutions. "Statement of Cataloguing Principles." The Hague: International Federation of Library Associations and Institutions, 2009b. http://www.ifla.org/en/publications/ statement-of-international-cataloguing-principles (accessed March 15, 2010).

International Federation of Library Associations and Institutions. "Statement of Principles." The Hague: International Federation of Library Associations and Institutions, 1961. http://www.d-nb.de/standardisierung/pdf/paris _principles_1961.pdf (accessed March 15, 2010).

Joint Steering Committee for Development of RDA. "A Brief History of AACR2." Joint Steering Committee for Development of RDA, July 2009. http://www.rda-jsc.org/history.html (accessed March 15, 2010).

Joint Steering Committee for Development of RDA. "Historic Documents: Outcomes of the Meeting of the Joint Steering Committee Held in Chicago, U.S.A., 24–28 April 2005." Joint Steering Committee for Development of RDA, May 2005. http://www.rda-jsc.org/0504out.html (accessed March 15, 2010).

Joint Steering Committee for Development of RDA. "RDA: Resource Description and Access: Frequently Asked Questions." Joint Steering Committee for Development of RDA. January 2010. http://www.rda-jsc.org/rdafaq.html (accessed March 15, 2010).

Kelm, Carol R. "The Historical Development of the Second Edition of the Anglo-American Cataloging Rules." *Library Resources & Technical Services* 22, no. 1 (1978): 22–33.

Knowlton, Steven A. "Criticism of Cataloging Code Reform, as Seen in the Pages of *Library Resources and Technical Services* (1957–66)." *Library Resources & Technical Services* 53, no. 1 (January 2009): 15–24.

LeVan, Ralph R. "Dublin Core and Z39.50." *Journal of Library Administration* 34, no. 3/4 (June 2001): 229–43.

Leyson, Joan M., and Jeanne M. K. Boydston. "Supply and Demand for Catalogers: Present and Future." *Library Resources & Technical Services* 49, no. 4 (October 2005): 250–65.

Libraries and Archives Canada. "Canadian Committee on Cataloguing." Ottawa: Libraries and Archives Canada, 2009. http://www.collections canada.gc.ca/cataloguing-standards/040006-3000-e.html (accessed May 1, 2010).

Library Association, Media Cataloguing Rules Committee. *Non-Book Materials Cataloguing Rules: Integrated Code of Practice and Draft Revision of the Anglo-American Cataloguing Rules, British Text, Part 3*. Working paper 11. London: National Council for Educational Technology, Library Association, 1973.

Library of Congress. *Rules for Descriptive Cataloging in the Library of Congress*. Washington, DC: Library of Congress, Descriptive Cataloging Division, 1949.

Lubetzky, Seymour. "Code of Cataloging Rules: Author and Title Entry. Introduction." In *Seymour Lubetzky: Writings on the Classical Art of Cataloging*, ed. Elaine Svenonius and Dorothy McGarry, 209–17. Englewood, CO: Libraries Unlimited, 2001.

Martell, Charles. "The War of AACR2: Victors or Victims?" *Journal of Academic Librarianship* 7, no. 1 (1981): 4–8.

Martin, Susan K. "A Learning Experience." *American Libraries* 11, no. 2 (February 1980): 117–18.

Maxwell, Margaret F. "Guidelines for a Future Anglo-American Cataloging Code." In *The Future of Cataloging*, ed. Tschera Harkness Connell and Robert L. Maxwell, 157–62. Chicago: American Library Association, 2000.

Maxwell, Robert L. *Maxwell's Handbook for AACR2: Explaining and Illustrating the Anglo-American Cataloguing Rules through the 2003 Update*. 4th ed. Chicago: American Library Association, 2004.

Mayernik, Matthew. "The Distributions of MARC Fields in Bibliographic Records: A Power Law Analysis." *Library Resources & Technical Services* 54, no. 1 (2010): 40–54.

McCallum, Sally. "What Makes a Standard?" *Cataloging & Classification Quarterly* 21, no. 3–4 (1996): 5–15.

Merrett, Bronwen, and Anne Sedgley. "Cataloguing Slide Collections: Art and Architecture Slides at RMIT (Royal Melbourne Institute of Technology)." *Australian Library Journal* 23, no. 4 (1974): 146–52.

Pang, Isabel S. "How AACR 2 Will Affect a Medium-Sized Library." *Journal of Academic Librarianship* 6, no. 4 (1980): 208–9.

Patton, Glenn E., ed. *Functional Requirements for Authority Data: A Conceptual Model*. IFLA Series on Bibliographic Control, vol. 34. Munich: K. G. Saur, 2009.

Quinly, William J. *Standards for Cataloging Nonprint Materials*. 3rd ed. Washington, DC: Association For Educational Communications and Technology, 1972.

R.M.D. "Leaping into the Void." *Journal of Academic Librarianship* 6, no. 3 (July 1980): 131.

Ranganathan, S. R. *The Five Laws of Library Science*. New Delhi: Ess Ess Publications, 2006.

Schottlaender, Brian E. C., ed. *The Future of the Descriptive Cataloging Rules: Papers from the ALCTS Preconference, AACR2000, American Library Association Annual Conference, Chicago, June 22, 1995*. ALCTS Papers on Library Technical Services and Collections, no. 6. Chicago: American Library Association, 1998.

Schrader, Vivian L. "The Cataloging of Nonprint Media: A Challenge and the Revision of the Anglo-American Cataloging Rules to Meet the Challenge." Paper presented at the 25th biennial conference of Southwestern Library Association, Galveston, Texas, October 15, 1974.

Steinhagen, Elizabeth N., Mary Ellen Hanson, and Sharon A. Moynahan. "Quo Vadis, Cataloging?" *Cataloging & Classification Quarterly* 44, no. 3/4 (May 2007): 271–80.

Taylor, Arlene G., and Barbara Paff. "Looking Back: Implementing AACR 2." *The Library Quarterly* 56, no. 3 (1986): 272–85.

Texas A&M. "Speedy 'AACR 2' Switchover Logged by Texas A&M." *Library Journal* 106, no. 2 (February 1981): 408.

University of Illinois. "University of Illinois Switches to 'AACR 2.'" *Library Journal* 105, no. 1 (January 1980): 13–14.

Weihs, Jean R., ed. *The Principles and Future of AACR: Proceedings of the International Conference on the Principles and Future Development of AACR, Toronto, Ontario, Canada, October 23–25, 1997*. Ottawa: Canadian Library Association, 1998.

Wilder, Stanley J. "Demographic Trends Affecting Professional Technical Services Staffing in ARL Libraries." *Cataloging & Classification Quarterly* 34, no. 1/2 (2002): 53–57.

Wright, Wyllis. "The Anglo-American Cataloging Rules: A Historical Perspective." *Library Resources & Technical Services* 20, no. 1 (1976): 36–47.

Yee, Martha M. "What Is a Work?" In *The Principles and Future of AACR*, ed. Jean R. Weihs, 62–104. Ottawa: Canadian Library Association, 1998.

CHAPTER 2

Impact of Changes in Library of Congress Cataloging Policy on Working Catalogers

Bonnie Parks

The traditional practice of bibliographic control, the value of library catalogs, and the expenses that accompany them are currently under fire. This is not surprising in an environment of readily available technology and tough economic times. Information seekers want immediate results and popular search engines like Google and Yahoo!, and websites like Amazon.com have become the standards against which library catalogs are judged. Even within the library community, the relevance and necessity of Machine Readable Cataloging (MARC) records and the cost-effectiveness of cataloging have been called into question. Yet in an environment where key word searching is the norm, accurate description and controlled vocabulary still provide users with superior means to identify and select needed resources. Libraries do not need to sacrifice their cataloging efforts during budget crises. Instead, by participating in cooperative cataloging programs, libraries can reduce costs while still providing an effective and powerful catalog for their users.

The notion of maximizing the value of catalog records and cutting costs by sharing the products of our labor is not new. Catalogers enjoy a history of cooperation that dates back more than 100 years when the Library of Congress (LC) began its shared card program. More recently, bibliographic utilities such as the Online Computer Library Center (OCLC) have proved an invaluable resource for sharing MARC records. Another well-known cooperative effort, the Program for Cooperative Cataloging (PCC), is an international effort aimed at expanding access to library collections by providing useful, timely, and cost-effective cataloging that meets mutually accepted standards of libraries (http://www.loc.gov/catdir/pcc/MissionStatement.html).

LC is one of many PCC participants. LC serves on both the PCC Steering Committee and the Policy Committee. It operates as the secretariat to coordinate and support component programs within the PCC. Those programs include the Name Authority Cooperative Program (NACO), Bibliographic Record Cooperative Program (BIBCO), Cooperative Online Serials Program (CONSER), and the Subject Authority Cooperative Program (SACO). Staff at LC serve on PCC committees, task forces, and groups within the PCC and play key roles in many of the program's policies and practices. Along with catalogers at other institutions, catalogers at LC create bibliographic and authority records for distribution as PCC records for use by the library community (http://www.loc.gov/faq/catfaq.html). Recent cooperative efforts between LC and the PCC have been fueled by the need to make an increased number of materials available in a variety of formats without sacrificing quality and while working within the confines of tighter budgets.

Cataloging practitioners have had to address some of the policy decisions driven by these factors. LC's cessation of the creation and maintenance of series authority records and the implementations of the CONSER Standard Record, BIBCO Standard Record, and Provider-Neutral Record for monographs are four recent decisions that give cataloging operations cause to rethink their services and reevaluate their practices. The intent of this chapter is not to debate whether the arguments have merit or whether the expense of cataloging is justifiable. Instead, the author aims to address some of the recent changes in cataloging and coding practices and the reasoning behind the decisions and to provide practical guidance on incorporating these changes into daily work flow.

SERIES AUTHORITY RECORDS

Perhaps the policy change that has generated the greatest amount of dialogue in recent history is the LC's decision to stop creating series authority records (SARs). LC announced that as of May 1, 2006, its catalogers would no longer create SARs and cease to provide controlled series access in bibliographic records produced by its catalogers. Citing environmental changes—namely, more powerful indexing and key word access—LC decided that the processing time saved by its staff would outweigh any drawbacks resulting from lack of SAR production (e-mail from Les Hawkins to CONSERLST, "LC Series Authority Record Change," April 21, 2006). LC stated that the new policy, which went into effect June 1, 2006, would apply to all bibliographic resources (monographs, serials, and integrating resources).

Some argue that SARs serve important functions for both users and library staff. The SAR contains the authorized form of a given series and ensures that treatment is consistent for all items in the series and that the results of a series title search are collocated in the library catalog. A user can determine, after a single search, whether the library owns a given item in a particular series. SARs also enhance user access to materials by differentiating among series with similar titles. Library staff, too, benefit from SARs. For example, specific fields within the MARC record provide information about cataloging decisions such as treatment and classification. Whenever a new item in a series arrives, acquisitions staff and/or catalogers need only glance at the authority record to determine the treatment of that item. To adapt to this change, cataloging departments are adjusting their work flows and procedures. Catalogers have two options: follow either current LC practice or the methods prescribed by the PCC.

Current LC Practice

Current LC practice is reflected in the August 2009 revision of Library of Congress Rule Interpretation (LCRI) 13.3. The LCRI notes that LC analyzes and classifies separately all parts of monographic series and multipart monographs with a few exceptions. LC no longer includes " 'controlled' access points for series in new LC original cataloging (CIP and non-CIP), does not update series access points in existing bibliographic records, and does not consult, make, or update series authority records" (LCRI 13.3). LC now transcribes series information in field 490, first indicator 0. SARs no longer are created or maintained, and series data are not updated in existing bibliographic records. Analyzed sets and/or analyzed serials titles no longer are classified together. Rather, separate bibliographic records are created, and works are classified on the basis of their respective subjects. Additionally, LC creates separate bibliographic records for individual volumes of multipart monographs bearing analyzable titles.

Current PCC Practice

Members of the PCC continue to create and maintain SARs. An e-mail from the chair of the PCC Policy Committee (PoCo) outlined the PCC Steering Committee's decisions about how series would be treated. "Transcription of the series statement is mandatory if applicable," and searching for series authority records, tracing the series, and creating and maintaining SARs is optional (e-mail from Rebecca Mugridge, chair, PCC Policy Committee, August 22, 2008, sent to various PCC and non-PCC discussion lists.) This means that those PCC members who choose not to trace series can follow the LC practice of transcribing series statements in a BIBCO record in field 490 0#, but those who do exercise the option to trace series in bibliographic records are required to search the LC/NACO Authority File for authorized forms of series (http://www.loc.gov/catdir/pcc/bibco/seriesfaq.html).

New MARC Series Coding

In October 2008, MARC field 440 (series statement/added entry) was declared obsolete in favor of using field 490 (series statement) and the 8XX series added entry fields for traced series. Field 440 was used to record a series on a resource when the transcription from the resource was identical to the established form of the series. The field served double duty: it was a transcription field, and it provided an authorized added entry in the bibliographic record. MARC fields 800 to 830 are series added entry fields. They contain a name/title or a title used as a series added entry when the series statement is contained in MARC field 500 (general note) and a series added entry is wanted for the bibliographic record. Before field 440 became obsolete, MARC fields 800 to 830 were paired with field 490 to allow the transcription of an unauthorized form of a series (if it appeared on the piece in hand) while tracing the authorized form.

This example of the former practice shows a publication that appears in two series:

245   00   Renal problems in critical care / ‡c edited by Lynn Schoengrund, Pamela Balzer.

440   #0   Critical care nursing series [authorized form of series and appears on piece as such]

490   1#   A Wiley medical publication [series title as it appears on the piece]

830   #0   Wiley medical publication. [authorized form of series]

Making field 440 obsolete was a topic of discussion earlier and was suggested in 1989 as MARBI Proposal 89-7, although the proposal was not approved at that time. However, discussions focusing on simplifying practices for libraries and vendors that continue series work grew out of LC's 2006 series policy, and these discussions revived interest in the idea of eliminating field 440. MARC Discussion Paper 2008-DP02 was written and made available for comment in December 2007. The paper suggested making field 440 obsolete in favor of using field 490 (series statement) and the 8XX series added entry fields. Proponents argued that this would simplify practice and the need for systems to look multiple places in the records for the authorized series heading. It resulted in MARC Proposal No. 2008-07 the following year (http://www.loc.gov/marc/marbi/2008/2008 -dp02.html). Additional arguments in favor of the proposal reasoned that making field 440 obsolete would resolve the long-standing issue of field 440 being both a descriptive field and a controlled access point. Separation of the two functions would result in a more reliable description and, over time, easier authority control maintenance (http://www.loc.gov/marc/marbi/2008/2008-07.html). The proposal was approved in October 2008. At this writing, OCLC is in the process of converting existing 440 fields into the appropriate 490/830 combination, which will result in a standard application for all OCLC member libraries.

Current Practice (http://www.loc.gov/catdir/pcc/Field440.pdf)

Coding for MARC 21 field 490 first indicator definitions:

The definition of "0" has not changed, but a new definition for "1" is now valid.

1st indicator Series tracing policy. The series has no corresponding added entry (not traced) or has a corresponding 800–830 series added entry field (traced differently).

0—Series not traced   No series added entry is desired for the series.

1—Series traced in 8XX field.   When value "1" is used, the appropriate field 800–830 is included in the bibliographic record to provide the series added entry.

Examples of coding for field 490 taken from OCLC's *Bibliographic Formats and Standards*:

0   Series not traced. No series added entry is desired for the series.
490 0# Pelican books

[indicates that there is no 800–830 field in the bibliographic record]

1#Series traced. When value 1 is present, the appropriate 800–830 field (8XX fields) is included in the bibliographic record to provide the series added entry.

Examples of current practice:

490   1#   Department of State publication; ‡v 7846. ‡a Department and Foreign Service series ; ‡v 128

830   #0   Department of State publication; ‡v 7846.

830   #0   Department of State publication. ‡p Department and Foreign Service series ; ‡v 128

[The series statement contains a numbered series and a subseries, and both are to be traced separately.]

490   1#   Uniform crime reports

830   #0   Uniform crime reports (Washington, D.C.)

[The established form of entry for the series includes a parenthetical qualifier.] LC's decision to cease creating and maintaining SARs, coupled with MARBI's decision to render MARC field 440 obsolete, has forced libraries to consider whether they will continue to provide controlled access to series information or abandon the practice and rely on their local system's indexing to lead users to the resources they seek. There are several factors for cataloging managers to consider before making the series treatment decision that best suits their library's needs, including the following:

- Does your library create SARs as part of NACO?
- Are series verified and controlled at the point of cataloging?

- Do you outsource your authority control and/or any of your cataloging to a vendor, or are your authority records maintained in-house?
- Are traced series important to your users? (You will want to gather input from your public services librarians to determine the answer to this question.)
- Does your online catalog index all series, including untraced field 490 0#?

Practical Solutions

If you answered "yes" to any of the questions in the section above, consider the value of continuing to provide controlled series access to your users. You may need to modify your DLC cataloging work flow. Copy catalogers working with DLC copy should check for series statements in 490 0# fields and verify whether SARs already exist for those series statements. As with any change in procedure, there are initial investments in time and training to consider, but as the new workflow becomes part of the daily routine, the additional time spent diminishes.

Consider participating in NACO program of the PCC if your institution is not already doing so. Cataloging is a cooperative activity, and the shared effort to create and maintain SARs benefits not only individual institutions but also the larger cataloging community. One of the PCC's objectives in its 2007–2010 Strategic Directives includes exploring "a new category of membership that will allow individuals who do not work in a PCC member organization to contribute PCC records" (http://www.loc.gov/catdir/pcc/ stratdir-2008.html). This may be good news for catalogers who have PCC/ NACO experience but currently do not work in a PCC member organization. Recently, a trial membership of an individual who moved from a CONSER institution to a non-CONSER institution was arranged as an initial test of the feasibility of this objective (http://www.loc.gov/catdir/pcc/Details.html #SD3_Obj1_Act1). As of September 30, 2009, the CONSER experiment was considered successful and might be expanded. A few obstacles must be overcome before opening the program to other areas of PCC participation, but its future looks promising.

Even if your library is unable to participate in a national program like the PCC, continuing to provide series authority control in your local system is still a useful endeavor because it maintains a consistent approach to cataloging and helps preserve the integrity of existing records in your catalog. For those libraries that rely on an outside vendor for their authority records, ask whether they offer a service to flip the obsolete 440 fields into 490, first indicator 1, and corresponding 830 fields. The library vendors Backstage, MARCIVE, and LTI offer this type of service.

While it is still too soon to determine the long-term effects of LC's series treatment decision, it is not too early to adopt the new series standard now in order to prevent more cleanup work in the future. Likewise, it is never too early for libraries to reap the benefits of the expertise of PCC members. Libraries can adopt the above suggestions to whatever level best suits the needs of their staff and, ultimately, their users. The bibliographic universe will undoubtedly continue to shift and change, and participation in cooperative efforts like those of the PCC demonstrate a shared commitment to quality records produced in alignment with existing standards.

CONSER STANDARD RECORD

On June 1, 2007, the PCC's CONSER program implemented the CONSER Standard Record (CSR) for serials in all formats. Developed with the intention of meeting user needs an evolving digital environment, the CSR emphasizes access points rather than extensive descriptive detail in the belief that controlled subject and name access points are cataloging's most valuable contribution in the current bibliographic environment (CSR Documentation, July 22, 2009).

The project began in 2005. The working group charged with the development of this new "standard" record (formerly called the "access level record") agreed on three objectives to guide its decision-making process: functionality, cost-effectiveness, and conformity to current standards (http://www.loc.gov/acq/conser/alrFinalReport.html). Described as a "floor," not a "ceiling," the new record promotes an essential set of elements required to meet Functional Requirements for Bibliographic Records (FRBR) user tasks (find, identify, select, and obtain). Catalogers are free to exercise judgment and add additional elements not included in the essential element set if needed to meet specific FRBR user tasks required by the nature of the resource or the particular needs of an institution. Cost of the creation and maintenance of the records and the associated cataloger training should be less than the costs of creating full-level records. Finally, the group agreed that the rules used to create the new records should conform to current descriptive cataloging standards, subject access, and content designation (http://www.loc.gov/acq/conser/alrFinalReport.html).

This new standard record replaces full- and core-level CONSER records—encoding levels "blank" and "4," respectively. Minimal records (records encoded as level "7") are still permissible, although they are not considered CSRs. Many of the elements that catalogers expect in a serial record remain the same, including main entry, title proper, place of publication, publisher, current frequency, numbering area, subject headings, most linking fields, and added entries. The coding of some of the fixed field elements has been simplified, as has the coding of MARC fields 006 and 007 and indicators for field 246. Because of its emphasis on controlled access rather than transcription of descriptive elements, statements of responsibility and issuing body notes are no longer required as long as corporate body–added entries are backed by name authority records (NARs) in the LC/NACO Authority File.

Highlights and General Principles (from CSR Documentation July 22, 2009)

- CSRs use MARC 21 encoding level "blank" and LC/NACO and Subject Authority Files are required for all headings on CSRs.

- CSRs have an authentication code (MARC field 042) of "pcc." Records created prior to May 1, 2009, have authentication code "lc" or "lcd."

- All CSRs must contain at a minimum, the mandatory elements spelled out in the Metadata Application Profile (MAP) (http://www.loc.gov/catdir/cpso/conserdoc.pdf).

- Standard abbreviations and capitalization are no longer required in designation and notes fields (362, 515, 5XX).

- "Description Based On" information and source of title are required in all records and should be combined in a single note. (Exception: Source of title is not required for derived records.)

Records created prior to the implementation of the CSR do not have to be edited to conform to the new guidelines.

Documentation and Training

A number of excellent training sources are available. Familiarizing yourself with the standard will help you implement choices that best suit your library's needs:

- CSR documentation includes field-specific instructions, decision-making guidance, bibliographic record examples, and advice for working with copy and record maintenance. Up-to-date documentation is available on the CONSER website at http://www.loc.gov/acq/conser/issues.html#standard-rec.

- LC's Policy and Standards Division has provided new or revised LCRIs to support policy decisions that differ from rules of the second edition of the *Anglo-American Cataloguing Rules*.

- The Serials Cooperative Cataloging Training Program (SCCTP) has created half-day CSR training workshops. Instruction is offered both remotely and in person. See the SCCTP website at http://www.loc.gov/acq/conser/scctp/scctp -home.html for more information.

Practical Solutions

Utilize existing documentation and incorporate it into your local procedures and work flow. Take advantage of available training opportunities that are offered in your area. Attending a local or regional workshop can be an inexpensive way to manage changes. SCCTP, mentioned earlier, is a well-known and respected training source for serials cataloging-related instruction. Trainers for the program are experienced professionals, and the workshop materials are routinely updated to reflect current practice. In addition to the half-day workshop on the CSR, SCCTP offers a number of other serials cataloging-related workshops. Many organizations sponsor training sessions either as preconferences or as independent workshops. Organizations such as the North American Serials Interest Group routinely offer SCCTP workshops as preconferences. Regional and state library associations also tend to offer workshops at their annual meetings. In response to the needs of those who are not able to travel, many existing workshops—including courses by OCLC and those under the umbrella of the Catalogers Learning Workshop, including Cataloging for the 21st Century, Cooperative Cataloging Training, and SCCTP—are being adapted for distance learning. Often, the costs of the workshops are deliberately kept low to encourage participation.

BIBCO STANDARD RECORD

Following the success of the CSR, the PCC Steering Committee designated a Task Group on BIBCO Standard Record Requirements. Using the BIBCO core-level record as its starting point, the group's charge was to develop a model for print monograph records utilizing a single encoding level. As the CSR did with serials, this new standard record for print monographs would replace the preexisting BIBCO core (encoding level "4") and full (encoding level "blank") records. The Task Group was motivated, for in the span of a single year, documentation for the BIBCO Standard Record (BSR) and its accompanying MAP were created, and records were tested and submitted for review by the BIBCO community. On January 4, 2010, the BSR was implemented for print monographs including, nonelectronic reproductions.

The BSR shares a likeness with its predecessor the CSR. The BSR is described as a "floor" record that has been designed to meet the FRBR user tasks. In other words, it is a basic record that can be further enhanced to >benefit users. As with the CSR, the BSR emphasizes access points over extensive descriptive data. Catalogers are free to exercise judgment and add additional elements essential to meeting FRBR user tasks that might be required by the nature of the resource or the particular needs of an institution.

Highlights and General Principles

- BSRs use MARC 21 encoding level "blank."
- Main entry headings (1XX), added entries (7XX), and subject headings (6XX) are supported by LC/NACO and SACO programs
- BSRs have an authentication code (MARC field 042) of "pcc."
- All BSRs contain, at a minimum, the mandatory elements spelled out in the MAP.

Documentation and Training

- The BSR MAP includes field-by-field guidance. Up-to-date documentation is available on the BIBCO home page (http://www.loc.gov/catdir/pcc/bibco).

- The Standing Committee on Training (SCT) plans to develop training documentation.

- OCLC has expressed a willingness to work with the PCC to present a Web-based training session for OCLC member libraries.

Although the BSR model exists only for print monographs at this time, the PoCo has charged the Standing Committee on Standards with developing models to extend the BSR to electronic books, rare books, and monographs in nonbook formats.

Practical Solutions

Take advantage of existing documentation and integrate it into local procedures and work flow. Seek out available training opportunities for your cataloging staff. An initial investment in training can save your library time and money in the long run. Like the CSR, the BSR shows promise to be more cost effective than cataloging according to the former full-level standard. Remember, it is PCC policy that all new BIBCO records are created according to the new standard. Catalogers in non-BIBCO libraries are encouraged to catalog according to the new standard. In addition, remember that the BSR is a "floor" record. As such, it is flexible and allows catalogers to add more data, especially in areas where they have special expertise or with materials of particular significance to their collections.

PROVIDER-NEUTRAL RECORD FOR E-MONOGRAPHS

Another recent policy change within the cooperative cataloging community is the adoption of the Provider Neutral Record for e-monographs. The concept of a single bibliographic record covering all manifestations of an online resource was first proposed at the CONSER Operations Committee (OpCo) meeting in May 2002 as the Aggregator-Neutral Record for serials (http://www.loc.gov/acq/conser/singleonline.html). Serials catalogers were looking for an easier way to address the presentation of identical content by multiple aggregators. Multiple bibliographic records for each provider proved to be confusing to users and difficult for catalogers to maintain. The proposal was discussed during the spring and summer of 2002, input was gathered, and the Aggregator-Neutral Record for serials was implemented in July 2003 (http://www.loc.gov/acq/conser/conop2003.html). OCLC ran a global automated process to remove duplicate records from the utility.

The concept of a provider-neutral record for online monographs was discussed at the 2008 BIBCO OpCo meeting, and the Provider-Neutral E-Monograph Record Task Group was formed following the 2008 American Library Association annual conference. The group's charge was to develop a provider-neutral record model for use with all instances of an online monograph, and its model and accompanying report were approved by the PoCo and announced on April 30, 2009 (e-mail from Les Hawkins to OCLC-Cataloging [OCLC-CAT@OCLC.ORG] June 11, 2009). The new guidelines went into effect in August 2009 and apply to all PCC member libraries coding their records as PCC program records (MARC field 042 pcc) whenever they create or revise master records in OCLC. Adoption of this policy should make the cataloging treatment of these resources more consistent and eliminate redundancies and future duplicate records from OCLC.

OCLC member libraries may edit and replace master records to reflect the new guidelines. OCLC plans to match and merge straightforward duplicate records in a global duplicate detection process in 2010 (e-mail from Robert Bremer to PCCLIST, August 13, 2009). Until the initial match and merge process is completed, OCLC recommends that catalogers report only duplicate records that are unlikely to be caught in an automated match process.

Highlights and General Principles

- The provider-neutral e-monograph record emphasizes recording information that applies to all e-manifestations of a resource. Notes and added entries should not be created for specific packages, as the goal of the record is to remain as neutral as possible.
- Multiple URLs may be recorded in the bibliographic record for packages that contain full text.
- Electronic resources are not considered to be reproductions, so MARC field 533 (reproduction note) no longer will be used, except for digital preservation projects.
- The publisher and dates will be for those of the original monograph, not for the digitizer and dates of digitization.
- MARC field 300 in these records will begin with "1 online resource."

Documentation and Training

- The Provider-Neutral E-Monograph Record MARC Record Guide includes field-by-field guidance (http://www.loc.gov/catdir/pcc/bibco/PN-Guide.pdf).
- Ten sample provider-neutral records are available in OCLC and are retrievable with the title search "Provider Neutral Task Force (PCC) example records."

Practical Solutions

The new provider-neutral policy draws on an already existing policy for serials and integrating resources that has increased cataloging efficiency by eliminating the need to create an original bibliographic record for the same intellectual content when it appears in different packages. Maintaining a single bibliographic record for all versions of the same resource not only provides better user access but also saves the library time and money. Original catalogers can take advantage of the existing documentation and sample records that are available from the PCC website to create local procedures. Libraries using OCLC as their bibliographic utility have been instructed to cease creating provider-specific bibliographic records, and OCLC member libraries can edit and replace master records for e-monographs. This means that the types of records catalogers encounter in Connexion increasingly will reflect the new policies.

Some of the recent changes in cataloging and coding practices have been addressed in this chapter along with the reasoning behind the decisions. Practical guidance is provided on taking advantage of existing documentation and training opportunities to incorporate these changes into daily work flow. In particular, this chapter offers assistance with coping with LC's cessation of the creation and maintenance of series authority records, the implementations of the CONSER Standard Record, BIBCO Standard Record, and Provider-Neutral Record for monographs. By evaluating the impact of these changes on departmental work flow, catalogers can begin to adjust their practices to continue providing consistent and reliable access to their library's resources. Not only is sharing cooperatively created records cost effective, as the energy and expertise is distributed among many libraries, but cooperative cataloging allows libraries to add records that adhere to current standards in less time than it would take if the library were operating on its own. By taking advantage of cooperative cataloging efforts, such as those of the PCC, libraries can weather the current economic crisis while simultaneously providing high-quality cataloging and easy access to their users. A Haitian proverb says, "Men anpil, chay pa lou," which means, "Many hands lighten the load." When libraries make a commitment to work together, everyone benefits.

BIBLIOGRAPHY

BIBCO (Program). "BIBCO Home." http://www.loc.gov/catdir/pcc/bibco (accessed December 22, 2009).

BIBCO (Program). "Provider-Neutral E-Monograph Record Task Group Report, July 30, 2009." http://www.loc.gov/catdir/pcc/bibco/PN-Final-Report.pdf (accessed December 22, 2009).

CONSER Operations Committee. "CONSER Operations Committee Annual Meeting, May 1–3, 2003 Summary." http://www.loc.gov/acq/conser/conop2003.html (accessed December 22, 2009).

CONSER Program. "Access Level Record for Serials Working Group Final Report." http://www.loc.gov/acq/conser/alrFinalReport.html (accessed December 22, 2009).

CONSER Program. "CONSER Standard Record Documentation 7/22/09." http://www.loc.gov/catdir/cpso/conserdoc.pdf (accessed December 22, 2009).

CONSER Program. "Serials Cataloging Issues: CONSER Standard Record." http://www.loc.gov/acq/conser/issues.html (accessed December 22, 2009).

CONSER Program. "Single Records for Online Versions of Print Serials." http://www.loc.gov/acq/conser/singleonline.html (accessed December 22, 2009).

Library of Congress. "Library of Congress Frequently Asked Questions: Cataloging at the Library of Congress." http://www.loc.gov/faq/catfaq.html (accessed December 22, 2009).

Library of Congress. *Library of Congress Rule Interpretations*. August 2009. http://www.loc.gov/catdir/cpso/lcri13_3.pdf (accessed December 21, 2009).

MARBI. "MARC Discussion Paper No. 2008-DP02." http://www.loc.gov/marc/marbi/2008/2008-dp02.html (accessed December 21, 2009).

MARBI. "MARC Proposal No. 2008-07." http://www.loc.gov/marc/marbi/2008/2008-07.html (accessed December 21, 2009).

OCLC. "Bibliographic Formats and Standards." http://www.oclc.org/bibformats/default.htm (accessed December 22, 2009).

Program for Cooperative Cataloging. "Details from the Strategic Directions for the Program for Cooperative Cataloging (PCC)." http://www.loc.gov/catdir/pcc/Details.html (accessed December 22, 2009).

Program for Cooperative Cataloging. "Frequently Asked Questions about Series." http://www.loc.gov/catdir/pcc/bibco/seriesfaq.html (accessed December 22, 2009).

Program for Cooperative Cataloging. "PCC Guidelines for Field 440." http://www.loc.gov/catdir/pcc/Field440.pdf (accessed December 22, 2009).

Program for Cooperative Cataloging. "PCC Mission Statement, 2005." http://www.loc.gov/catdir/pcc/MissionStatement.html (accessed December 22, 2009).

Serials Cataloging Cooperative Training Program. "Serials Cataloging Cooperative Training Program (SCCTP)." http://www.loc.gov/acq/conser/scctp/scctp-home.html (accessed December 22, 2009).

CHAPTER 3

Managing a Multiplicity of Standards: Hybrid Approaches to Traditional and Digital Cataloging

Kevin Clair and Robert Freeborn

Not long ago, in a galaxy very similar to this one, a library was a building that housed books. A librarian would purchase either new or replacement books, and then they (or another librarian if the library was large enough) would create catalog cards for each book. These cards served two purposes. First, they allowed patrons to find the books much quicker than by browsing the entire collection, and, second, they informed administrators as to how many books were actually owned by the library. Time passed, and the library began purchasing other formats besides books. Still more time passed, and the card catalogs were replaced by electronic databases known as "online public access catalogs" (OPACs). However, even with these changes, the library itself was basically still the same; it was a building that contained a specific collection of physical items that were in turn represented by locally created catalog records.

That is when the world turned upside down. The amount of information available exploded almost overnight, and it was virtually impossible for the library to own (let alone house) all of it. So libraries purchased "access" to various offsite databases to cover a range of topics. They also purchased or created "born digital" materials that lived happily somewhere in cyberspace. All the while, physical items continued to pour into the library, and the poor librarians now had to provide access to all of it. What to do? How were they going to represent all these resources in the catalog? Better yet, *could* all these resources be represented by a single catalog? Was there possibly a better way? This chapter looks at both traditional and recent approaches to cataloging these myriad materials and offers a few insights on how to utilize both of them in a single library setting.

TRADITIONAL CATALOGING STRATEGIES

In the traditional world, digital materials are treated are very similarly to their physical brethren. One would either create a bibliographic record according to the second edition of the *Anglo-American Cataloguing Rules* (AACR2) and the Machine Readable Cataloging (MARC) standards or (if one had access) search the WorldCat database run by the Online Computer Library Center (OCLC) for an appropriate record to copy. Some libraries will often add a note concerning the digital item to the record for its physical counterpart. The advantage of this is that the user can easily find all the available formats for a particular title in one record. Problems, however, can occur if the physical format is ever withdrawn from the catalog for whatever reason, requiring either creation of a new record for the digital item or the editing of the current record to reflect the physical item's absence. Since the item does not physically exist, many libraries will assign all digital items a single call number and allow the OPAC to automatically generate a bar code (see Example 1). This approach does nothing in terms of accessibility, except perhaps to identify all digital resources in the catalog, but is required because of the current requirements of most catalogs.

There are several advantages and disadvantages to handling digital materials in a traditional manner. AACR2 and MARC are firmly established in the library community and have been adapted to handle a wide variety of formats. Aside from official organs such as the American Library Association, the Library of Congress, and OCLC, there are many other groups at the national, regional, and local levels that can provide support for a vast number of

EXAMPLE 1

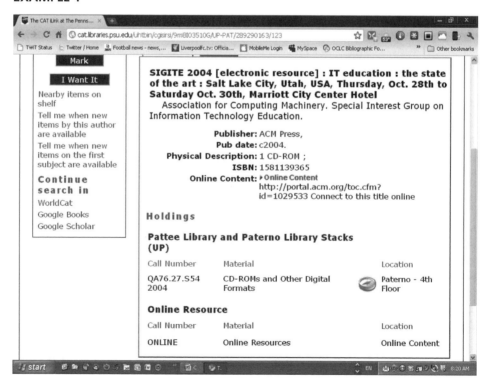

cataloging challenges (see Example 2). This is extremely beneficial to librarians because the traditional cataloging rules, while providing a firm foundation on which to build a bibliographic record, often leave decisions open to various interpretations. While this allowance for "cataloger judgment" is a good thing, some librarians would prefer to have additional guidance. The disadvantage of AACR2 and MARC is that they are not standards normally seen outside the libraries, creating a rather insular and artificial worldview of the overall information community. The creators of AACR2 have tried to rectify this situation by creating a new generation of the rules, named *Resource Description and Access* (RDA). Scheduled to be published in 2010, it is hoped that RDA will become a standard not only within the library world but beyond as well. However, it is too early to know whether RDA will achieve this.

Another advantage is the previously mentioned WorldCat database run by OCLC. Comprised of millions of bibliographic and authority records, WorldCat saves hundreds of thousands of librarians the time and effort of personally creating catalog records by allowing them to search and download the appropriate titles directly to their catalogs. They can also add to WorldCat on those occasions when the right record cannot be found, in turn assisting their fellow colleagues by saving them time and effort. There have been, however, two major disadvantages to WorldCat. One is that duplicate records for the same item often appear, and the other is the variation in

EXAMPLE 2

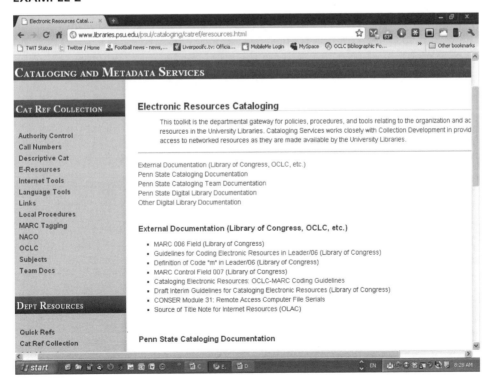

EXAMPLE 2 [CONT.]

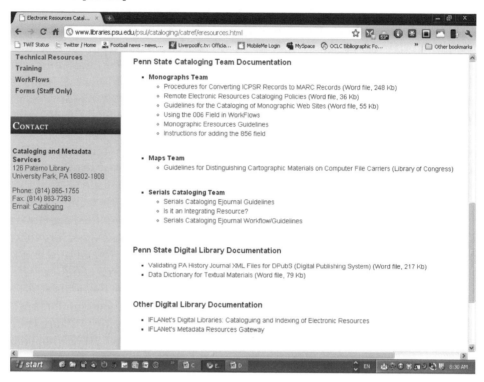

quality of cataloging contributed by members, some of which is substandard if not erroneous. While OCLC has tried to address these problem records, the task is just too vast for their staff. Member libraries have been enlisted to assist with quality control through such programs as Enhance and most recently the Expert Community project, but the problem is still a difficult one to overcome.

It should also be noted that, while the majority of WorldCat records are based on AACR2 and MARC, OCLC has been involved in integrating metadata from other sources and in other standards, such as CONTENTdm records marked up in Dublin Core. Additionally, after the move to RDA, WorldCat will contain records encoded according to both sets of cataloging rules, as adoption will occur in phases and some libraries will continue to create records using AACR2. This means that in the next decade or two, the makeup of the WorldCat database could be significantly changed; it will certainly include a greater diversity of formats and rules than it does now.

AACR2 and MARC also create records with a deep level of data granularity. By utilizing authority control and established subject thesauri, experienced searchers can obtain much more accurate results than through key words alone. The disadvantage is that today's users are not willing to learn these searching "tricks of the trade" and are quite happy to accept whatever a simple key word search retrieves. It appears that integrated library system vendors believe this as well, creating front-end library catalog interfaces that eschew advanced searching in favor of the single-line key word entry and the user-generated tag cloud. A tag or word cloud is a visual model comprised on user-created keywords for a particular topic or item. The more often a key word has been chosen by the user, the larger that word becomes with the model. While these clouds can be very useful, they can also cause confusion to the searcher. They are still key word based, which can severely limit one's search results without meaningful connections between key word indices and authorized subject headings. Initiatives such as WorldCat Identities have done a good deal of work in linking authorized headings with key word searches and tag clouds, but there is much more work to be done to make such initiatives widely adopted.

DIGITAL LIBRARY METADATA: A SHORT HISTORY

While all this has been occurring, there has been a dramatic increase in both the quantity of digital library collections created by academic and research libraries and the amount of material in electronic formats purchased by them. These trends have changed the amount of metadata created by research libraries, the attributes that it describes, and in some cases the source of that metadata. This has changed the necessary skills for creating metadata in research library settings and the locations in which that metadata creation occurs.

With the proliferation of digital library resources concurrent with the growth of the Internet, there was a need for metadata conforming with Web standards yet able to address the distinct data management needs of libraries and other cultural institutions. The Dublin Core Metadata Initiative, a response to this problem, has been active since the mid-1990s and serves as the basis for a variety of metadata applications inside and outside the library community, but it sacrifices many of the specific applications relevant to catalogers in the interest of being as widely adoptable as possible across many communities of practice. A need emerged for more extensively defined metadata formats useful for libraries in their own digitization programs.

It was to this end that the Metadata Encoding and Transmission Standard (METS) and the Metadata Object Description Schema (MODS) were developed in the early part of the twenty-first century. METS was developed as a "package" format intended to store many different metadata formats; in a digital library context, this usually consists of descriptive, preservation, and technical metadata. MODS serves as a descriptive metadata format, analogous to (but not strictly meant to replace) MARC21. Both formats are compatible with XML. In recent years, a number of other metadata formats have emerged running parallel to or derived directly from the work of the METS and MODS formats; these include the PREMIS standard for preservation metadata and the MIX standard for technical metadata for digital images.

As libraries began to create more XML-encoded records describing their digital resources, the need to make those records available outside institution-specific repository silos quickly became apparent. This need was addressed in large part by the Open Archives Initiative, which developed the Protocol for Metadata Harvesting (OAI-PMH). Utilizing Dublin Core as its basis for metadata interoperability, OAI-PMH was quickly adopted among libraries and other cultural institutions as the basis for making metadata quickly and easily shareable, and shared metadata initiatives such as the Pennsylvania Digital Library now rely on it for building virtual collections. The Aquifer project, from the Digital Library Federation, served the same purpose but it used MODS as the base format for harvesting metadata.

Digital libraries today stand at the crossroads of many trends within librarianship and cultural institutions generally. These trends include the following:

- The move, if not away from MARC, then at the least toward combining it with other library-specific metadata formats and emerging Web standards, such as RDF
- The growing convergence in collection development and access missions among libraries, archives, and museums and the recognition that cultural institutions and their metadata are better together than apart
- The growing role of libraries as content creators and the awareness that metadata within the context of digital projects are often not the same as describing those same resources within cataloging departments or archival processing units

NEW APPROACHES

The architect Eliel Saarinen is quoted as saying that, in designing any object, one must consider it in its next-largest context. Although he was speaking of building and urban design, the same principle applies to the library catalog and underscores the importance of rethinking our approaches. The library catalog as it was initially conceived—a store of metadata concerning only those items the library owned and held within its walls—does not scale to the Internet and the many types of electronic resources owned and now created by the library. Digital initiatives and electronic resources mean that the library catalog—and anywhere else where library metadata might be located—is now located throughout the Web in any number of places; it is no longer confined to materials located on library shelves as it was before.

New Roles

It was largely in response to these challenges that the role of the metadata librarian in the research library was created. Generally, the basic respon-sibility of the metadata librarian is to provide cataloging for "digital resources," which may mean anything from electronic databases to institutional repository content to resources in digital collections and any combination thereof. They are often responsible for cataloging in non-MARC metadata formats, such as METS or MODS. Not all metadata librarians are responsible for these tasks in the same proportions of their daily work, and not all of them are cataloging exclusively in non-MARC, but the philosophy underlying their work is consistent across most if not all institutions that employ them.

John Chapman (2007, 279–85) has written about the role of metadata librarians in research libraries. Chapman's analysis positions the metadata librarian between the roles of traditional catalogers (to describe resources) and digital collection curators and managers (to make those resources available in a digital environment). He further expands this position, noting the four primary roles of metadata librarianship—collaboration, research, education, and development. These roles are intertwined with each other: research into new standards and practices lead to development of new processes and education of library faculty and staff, in turn begetting new research.

The role of collaboration in metadata librarianship and in hybrid approaches to cataloging is particularly interesting, as this collaboration can take on many forms. Chapman focuses on two aspects of collaboration—at an institutional level between the metadata librarian and the technical services units of the library and at a national level among other research institutions (including but by no means limited to other academic libraries). Such collaboration already exists among peer institutions and is well documented, for example, in the activities of the various Digital Library Federation Aquifer project working groups (Kott et al. 2006).

The trouble with digital project metadata is that it often requires metadata far beyond what a traditional MARC record would contain simply to serve researchers. Particular forms and genres require type-specific metadata, such as an audiovisual document with time stamps to indicate where a particular passage begins and ends. Digital collections with a particular subject focus could require the development of taxonomies specific to the needs of the collection's primary users, developed using the shared expertise of metadata experts and faculty or researchers in the topic area. Additionally, much of the metadata that make digital library projects functional will never be seen directly by digital library users. This includes description such as geocoding, METS structural metadata for page-turning applications, and rules for digital object preservation. Catalogers have always done this to some extent, utilizing the 5xx MARC fields, but metadata for digital library applications greatly extend this work. Such tasks can easily overwhelm any traditional cataloging tasks with which the metadata librarian is charged.

New Work Flows

Because digitization blurs the boundaries between departments within the library and between geographically separate institutions outside of it, collaborations across those boundaries become quite natural. To be sure, such collaboration has been taking place within libraries for a long time; witness the various Program for Cooperative Cataloging initiatives shepherded by the Library of Congress or WorldCat itself. Digitization—and, arguably to a greater extent, budget cuts and reductions in available resources—has accelerated this trend and opened libraries up to the possibilities of collaboration with other partners.

The HathiTrust is a highly visible example of this trend. Seeking to be the shared repository, at first only for Committee on Institutional Cooperation partner institutions and later for other institutions, such as the University of California, the HathiTrust has led in a variety of initiatives related to this mission.

Libraries have also begun to look "upstream" in the publishing process for sources of original cataloging. OCLC has partnered with a handful of publishers on a "next-generation cataloging" initiative that seeks to leverage the ONIX metadata created by publishers and vendors to describe their books internally to reduce the amount of original cataloging needed from library catalogers and improve the quality of publisher-sourced metadata (OCLC 2009).

New Technologies

To increase the utility of library metadata for as many researchers as possible, it is important to place it in as many potential content entry points as possible. To this end, a number of services have emerged on the Web. The most notable of these are WorldCat itself as well as the OAI-PMH, which powers metadata harvesting services such as OAIster. These allow for exporting metadata out of digital content management systems used by research libraries, such as CONTENTdm or Fedora, and into shared digital library services, such as the Pennsylvania Digital Library (http://padl.pitt.edu). These initiatives, while undoubtedly important, are still somewhat limited to the world of libraries, archives, and (to a lesser but growing extent) museums. Other data storage and sharing initiatives, developed within the Web standards community, have the potential of opening up library metadata as never before.

The linked data movement is the best example of this. Linked data is the most visible component of the semantic Web, which envisions the Internet less as a "web of documents" or pages connected by links using HTML than as a "web of data," that is, discrete data sets described using Web standards. In an essay, Tim Berners-Lee (2006), the originator of the linked data concept, outlines its four main rules:

1. Use URIs as names for things.
2. Use HTTP URIs so that people can look up those names.
3. When someone looks up a URI, provide useful information, using Web standards.
4. Include links to other URIs so that they can discover more things.

These rules, while grounded in Web standards terminology, may nonetheless look familiar to catalogers. Analogues may be found in OCLC numbers and ISBNs (URIs), the use of MARC as a descriptive standard (RDF), and the use of Z39.50 to query this data from multiple data sets (SPARQL, a language used to query RDF tables). Linked data's true value comes in the fourth rule, that is, the links to other URIs. In the linked data universe, a user pursuing a query on "Moby Dick" would be able to link to further information about Melville, whaling, British literature, other volumes from the publisher of the particular FRBR expression being described, and so on using the links in the record. These links are expressed as RDF "triples," which are essentially logical sentences (composed of "subject," "predicate," and "object") embodying the attributes associated with a resource. In short, where a MARC record would indicate that a monograph with ISBN 0679600108 would have as the contents of the 245 field the string "Moby Dick," RDF would indicate the same information as follows:

<urn:isbn:0679600108> <http://purl.org/dc/terms/title> "Moby Dick"

Linked data's usefulness increases as these RDF tables grow and include more data sets encoded in it. The current state of linked data is a mishmash of various RDF-encoded data sets, linked in a fairly haphazard way (see Example 3). This graph is undoubtedly confusing, even perhaps to those who make their living making sense of the linked data landscape. Moreover, since many of these data sets were constructed independently of each other, they contain differently worded terms to describe the same general concepts. This is a feature of the system rather than a bug, as Clay Shirky (2005) notes in "Ontology Is Overrated:" as more tags are created, signal loss from compressing concepts into a single categorization system is minimized, increasing the utility of the entire system. A handful of data and metadata librarians are already active in the area of linked data. Most visibly, the Library of Congress has made the *Library of Congress Subject Headings* available as linked data at http://id.loc.gov, with more authority files promised in the future. Metadata librarians will undoubtedly become more active in the linked data world in the future.

PROSPECTIVE SOLUTIONS

We have seen that the traditional rules of cataloging are being pressured to change on all sides, from changing user expectations for our catalogs to the disparate metadata needs of digital libraries and new channels of scholarly communication to the new standards associated with linked data and the semantic Web. Libraries have had success in meeting these new challenges through novel collaboration efforts and the creation of new digital cataloging

EXAMPLE 3

Source: http://linkeddata.org (accessed December 14, 2009).

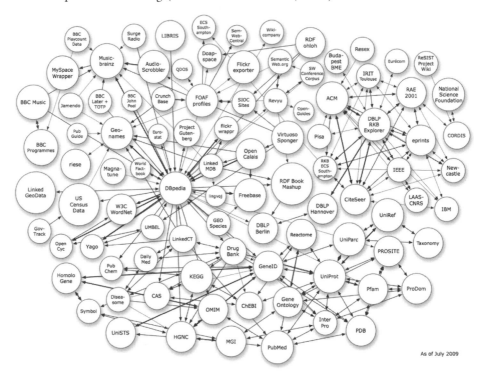

As of July 2009

roles, such as the metadata librarian. Clearly, this will not be enough to cope with accelerating digital transitions in publication of resources and of user behavior. There are some strategies that may gain currency going forward as a way to handle the changing cataloging landscape.

Chapman's (2007) article notes the importance of education and development of work flows in metadata librarianship; this role can easily be extended to outsourcing metadata creation to other departments or units in the cataloging department, allowing metadata librarians to focus on developing work flows and standards for new digital projects as old processes become routine. For example, many libraries are digitizing Sanborn fire insurance map collections, and the types of metadata required to make such projects successful are highly specific; they include things like accurate place-names, geocoding for coordinate points, and so forth. Such cataloging, once map digitization projects become a standard process, can be given to map cataloging teams. One of the roles of a metadata librarian, working in multiple standards, is to provide training for catalogers accustomed to working in MARC and AACR2 cataloging in the practices of non-MARC standards and linked data vocabularies. This distribution of nontraditional cataloging practice across library cataloging departments (and, ultimately, across departments) allows the metadata librarian to focus on more efficient uses of their skill set, such as taxonomy development and XSLT programming.

There are many adaptations that the library catalog can make to account for the upswing in digital materials it now contains and the changing searching behavior of users. Acknowledging that users will always want to search for key words and will not necessarily be aware of specific Library of Congress subject headings is an important step to take. A number of social cataloging theories and initiatives, such as the HathiTrust's Collection Builder utility or the "concept-oriented catalog" introduced and elaborated on by John Mark Ockerbloom (2009) in a recent series of blog posts, serve as powerful topic-oriented entry points from which users may be able to locate any number of resources—some of which may be hidden in current cataloging systems—helpful to them in answering their questions. Linked data can make this possible by connecting existing taxonomies (such as the Library of Congress subject headings) to similar taxonomies encoded in linked data, allowing library catalogs to connect with other data sets in other disciplines.

Contending with this changing landscape is as much a problem for cataloging department managers as it is for metadata librarians. While integrating metadata in the catalog with data practices on the Web is essential to ensuring that our metadata are accessible to as many users as possible, it is difficult to bring this work into the day-to-day operations of the cataloging department, especially as resources are scarce and it is increasingly difficult to bring in new staff to work exclusively on these issues. One possible solution is to take a project-based approach, similar to the way in which many libraries first approached digitization initiatives. When a digital project is in early stages—or even when a digitization program is first being initiated—it is worthwhile to identify the strengths of various staff or teams within the cataloging department and which of those strengths may apply to the metadata creation process. For example, a map cataloging team or a cataloger with particular expertise in map cataloging will be good at place-name authority control, identifying coordinate points, and similar tasks. These are useful skills for building geographic and map-based entry points to digital collections, which users are familiar with and which may bring in visitors that may not have otherwise discovered certain collections or objects. Working with the metadata librarian, cataloging managers can ensure that such skills are efficiently employed and that metadata skills are distributed across the cataloging department.

While admittedly uncertain, the future of the library catalog in the Internet age is exciting. Drawing on the rich set of metadata that already exist to describe library resources and utilizing the existing and evolving skill sets of both metadata specialists and traditional catalogers, we have already seen a number of initiatives emerge to enrich library catalogs and connect their data with the data sets elsewhere on the Internet. By encouraging collaborative efforts, distributed (and social) metadata production to describe library resources, and closer work with our colleagues in other cultural institutions, the library catalog can be well positioned as an information retrieval resource for our patrons.

BIBLIOGRAPHY

Berners-Lee, Tim. "Linked Data." 2006. http://www.w3.org/DesignIssues/LinkedData.html (accessed December 14, 2009).

Chapman, John. "The Roles of the Metadata Librarian in a Research Library." *Library Resources and Technical Services* 51, no. 4 (2007): 279–285.

Gorman, Michael, and Paul W. Winkler, eds., *Anglo-American Cataloguing Rules*. 2nd ed. Chicago: American Library Association, 1998.

Kott, Katherine, Jon Dun, Martin Halbert, Leslie Johnston, Liz Milewicz, and Sarah Shreeves. "Digital Library Federation (DLF) Aquifer Project." *D-Lib* 12, no. 5 (2006). http://www.dlib.org/dlib/may06/kott/05kott.html (accessed December 9, 2009).

Library of Congress Network Development and MARC Standards Office. *MARC Standards*. 2009. http://www.loc.gov/marc/marc.html (accessed December 14, 2009).

Ockerbloom, John Mark. "Understanding Concept-Oriented Catalogs." 2009. http://everybodyslibraries.com/2009/12/04/understanding-concept-oriented-catalogs (accessed December 15, 2009).

Online Computer Library Center. *Bibliographic Formats and Standards*. 4th ed. 2009. http://www.oclc.org/bibformats/default.htm (accessed December 14, 2009).

Shirky, Clay. "Ontology Is Overrated." 2005. http://www.shirky.com/writings/ontology_overrated.html (accessed February 15, 2010).

CHAPTER 4

Training Workshops: How One Trainer Works

Jay Weitz

In the years since I began working at Online Computer Library Center (OCLC) in 1982, the world of cataloging has changed, changed, and changed again. At that time, the conversion to the second edition of the *Anglo-American Cataloging Rules* (AACR2) was not merely fresh in catalogers' minds but was still actively underway in many institutions. Among my responsibilities at OCLC was serving as the cataloging specialist for what are lovingly referred to as the "funny formats," including scores, sound recordings, and visual materials.

In that era before the common availability of electronic mail and the Web, cataloging questions came to me via surface mail, phone calls, and biblio-graphic or authority record change requests. Catalogers would also ask their questions at meetings, conferences, or workshops. Regardless of the means of communication, though, the questions always had this in common: They arose in the course of everyday work and were asked so as to resolve a practical, pressing, real-time problem.

At the Music OCLC Users Group/Music Library Association (MOUG/MLA) meeting in Cleveland in March 1989, it was suggested that I start collecting and sharing these questions and answers with other catalogers in a column in the *MOUG Newsletter*. The first such column appeared in the *MOUG Newsletter* No. 39 in May 1989. In 2004, Libraries Unlimited published a collection of all those question-and-answer columns from 1989 to 2002 under the title *Cataloger's Judgment: Music Cataloging Questions and Answers from the Music OCLC Users Group Newsletter*. When Online Audiovisual Catalogers (OLAC) founder Nancy Olson decided to retire from writing her longtime question-and-answer column in the *OLAC Newsletter*, the editors asked for volunteers to step into Nancy's shoes. After submitting

---

Portions of this chapter have been adapted from a cataloging workshop presented as part of a preconference, "Cataloging Digital Media: Back to the Future," at the annual conference of the American Library Association, in Chicago, Illinois, on July 9, 2009.

my name for consideration, I was shocked at the uncharacteristic lack of judgment shown by the editors in accepting my submission. In 2004, I tried to pick up where Nancy had left off.

In short, for the better part of three decades—three decades in which the world of cataloging has remained in constant turmoil, from the AACR2 conversion spilling into the early 1980s, to Format Integration in the mid-1990s, to OCLC's transition from Passport software to its Connexion platform during the first decade of the 2000s, to the current ubiquity of electronic resources—I have been in the fortunate position of trying to answer the questions of catalogers who were dealing with that turmoil every day. From this vantage point and through these questions, I have watched as cataloging evolved, listened as catalogers' concerns changed, and marveled as unexpected issues arose. Those trying to keep catalogers informed have had to move with developments both within the realm of cataloging and in the larger world of the resources being cataloged.

During much that same period, beginning in 1992, I have put together a series of ever-evolving workshops on various aspects of cataloging, including scores, sound recordings, video recordings, electronic resources, and music uniform titles. In those nearly two decades, well over 40 workshop sessions have been presented across the United States and in Canada and Japan. The content of each workshop was determined by the questions that catalogers had asked me to address. With only a few exceptions, the structure and flow of each workshop were dictated by the participants and their questions. This helped assure that pressing, day-to-day questions tended always to be the focus of each workshop.

By the time that I was assembling my first workshops in the early 1990s, initially building on the work of OCLC colleagues, I already had a strong sense of the sorts of issues that concerned catalogers. From trying to answer their years of questions, I knew the areas of cataloging that caused the most confusion. It was around such general topics as physical descriptions, dates, differing formats, identifying numbers, sources of information, various types of notes, and the like that I began to build workshop lessons. Within these general topics, I tried to deal with the specific questions that arose time and time again. Whenever a new concern generated questions about a fresh area of cataloging—a new practice, a change to the Machine-Readable Cataloging (MARC) format, a revision to a rule—I knew it was time to address that in my workshop.

In most of my workshops, I take things one step further in a way that I have not seen other workshop leaders do. Following a standard introductory section, I open the floor to audience questions, the topics of which determine the direction of the workshop proper. This helps to ensure that the most pressing issues the attendees on any particular day are dealing with can get addressed. One disadvantage is that every workshop has its limits, so there is not time to address everyone's concerns.

In the introductory section, I deal with several basic topics that provide a common understanding among attendees and set a groundwork for everything that follows. We start with a few words about the relationship between the cataloging rules and the bibliographic format. The chief source of information and the prescribed sources of information for the particular bibliographic format are outlined. In the context of a cooperative database, decision points about when to create a new bibliographic record and when to use an existing record are discussed. Common ambiguities of bibliographic description that are found in records for materials of that particular type are emphasized, with hints about when to pay them attention and when to disregard them.

With this foundation established, questions are then welcome. Based on a knowledge of both the perennially troublesome areas of cataloging a particular type of material and the newer issues that may have arisen in recent months, I have prepared workshop sections on each and can skip to whichever of those topics comes up. For example, in my Videorecording Cataloging Workshop, there are sections on such topics as the physical description; the many dates associated with videos; the recording of and access to various kinds of intellectual, artistic, and technical responsibility; video presentation formats (full screen and letterboxing); dubbing, subtitling, captioning, and audio enhancement; the standard and other identifying numbers that can be found on videos; and so on.

Scattered throughout each workshop are full record examples that both highlight the particular issue at hand and put the results into their proper bibliographic context. My standard workshop handout is a compilation of all the bibliographic examples followed by a bibliography of useful resources both in print and online. The bibliographic examples used are sometimes the very records that brought the issue to the attention of the questioning cataloger. Many times, however, a clearer or more appropriate example can be found by some targeted searching through WorldCat. Today, the PowerPoint presentations of the workshops themselves are often made available online.

Serving as OCLC liaison to such groups as MOUG, OLAC, and the American Library Association's Map and Geography Round Table and answering cataloging questions are part of my job. But in this Internet-connected era, anyone who monitors a few of the major cataloging discussion lists over a period of time can get a good sense of catalogers' concerns, the things that are driving them nuts, and how they have chosen to deal with them.

One vivid and relatively recent example is that of the Playaway. This particular example is especially pertinent because it points up some of the shortcomings of both AACR2 and MARC and thus some of the reasons behind the impetus for a new set of cataloging rules and the need for a post-MARC bibliographic structure. Playaways describe themselves as a dedicated "self-playing digital audio book." Although it resembles such devices as the iPod, the Playaway contains a single preloaded audio file in a proprietary format known as Algebraic Code Excited Linear Prediction. Findaway World, the Ohio company that introduced the Playaway commercially in 2005, insists that the device cannot be hacked and will never be made programmable by users.

Not long after their commercial introduction, Playaways began to appear in libraries, proving especially popular in public libraries. Quickly, questions arose regarding how catalogers should deal with these unusual devices. Because of their hybrid nature as part sound recording, part electronic resource, Playaways seemed to be a perfect point of collaboration between OLAC's Cataloging Policy Committee and the MLA's Subcommittee on Descriptive Cataloging. Together, they formed the Playaway Cataloging Joint Task Force, which would draw up cataloging guidelines within the existing rules and bibliographic formats. The group did much of its work via e-mail but also met in person at several American Library Association conferences. In 2008, it produced the *Guide to Cataloging Playaway Devices Based on AACR2 Chapters 6* and *9* (http://www.olacinc.org/drupal/capc_files/playawaysPDF.pdf).

Throughout the ongoing computer revolution of recent decades, both AACR2 and MARC have often proven themselves to be remarkably adaptable to new and changing technologies. But the Playaway challenged long-established cataloging traditions in ways that highlighted the origins of AACR2 and MARC in a much simpler, more linear age. Nowhere was this more obvious than in the contentious, years-long debate over the proper General Material Designation (GMD) for the Playaway.

GMDs are the "early warning" device, in the form of a bracketed word or phrase, that AACR2 instructs catalogers to insert into the title statements of many bibliographic records. GMDs have their roots in a time when a sound recording was a sound recording was a sound recording and even when a computer file was a computer file was a computer file, and the twain did not meet. A bibliographic record can have only one GMD. Although both AACR2 and MARC have been fiddled with in order to allow multiple aspects of a single bibliographic resource to be expressed, it soon became clear that with the Playaway, the limits of GMD usefulness had been reached and exceeded.

Functionally, the Playaway is a "sound recording." But by the single-minded logic of AACR2, there was no choice but to assign the GMD "electronic resource." Public libraries were especially insistent that the "electronic resource" GMD would confuse their users. As a member of that Playaway Cataloging Joint Task Force, I heard the arguments on both sides within that group, then watched as the same arguments flew across several cataloging discussion lists on and off for more than two years.

Not only was the debate an education in its own right, but it also shed a bright light on the desperate need for a new approach to cataloging a world of previously unimaginable complexity. Calling into question the linear choice of a GMD for the Playaway, catalogers were calling out for a post-GMD mechanism that had the ability to express content, carrier, and medium simultaneously. Perhaps without knowing it, catalogers were pointing the way toward the new rules of Resource Description and Access (RDA) and corresponding additions to the MARC format that would accommodate a multifaceted replacement for the antiquated GMD. Likewise, they were taking into account the needs of library users, which sit at the heart of RDA's philosophical basis, the Functional Requirements for Bibliographic Records.

Playaways were part of the inspiration for a workshop to which I was asked to contribute as part of the preconference titled "Cataloging Digital Media: Back to the Future" at the annual conference of the American Library Association in Chicago, Illinois, on July 9, 2009. During 2008, OLAC had published two other sets of cataloging guidelines in addition to the previously mentioned Playaways document: *Guide to Cataloging DVD and Blu-ray Discs Using AACR2r and MARC 21: 2008 Update* (http://www.olacinc.org/drupal/capc_files/DVD_guide_final.pdf) and *Best Practices for Cataloging Streaming Media* (http://www.olacinc.org/drupal/capc_files/streamingmedia.pdf). Using elements of some of my own existing workshops and the three documents in question, I compiled a six-section workshop covering DVD-video, Blu-ray discs, DVD-audio, Playaways, DualDiscs, and streaming media.

Unlike many of my other workshops, this one had a set structure that did not lend itself to an open question-and-answer format. In each of the six sections, I dealt with a fairly standard list of important cataloging issues: a definition and description of the particular audiovisual medium, a brief history of the medium's development with an emphasis on when the medium was first made commercially available, and some of the basic coding and descriptive elements common to the medium (type of record, 007, GMD, the physical description, date peculiarities, any special notes, and so on). For the video media, I talked about identifying and recording such additional data as color broadcast systems, region information, aspect ratios, and sound characteristics.

Rather than using full bibliographic record examples, for this workshop I used only partial examples that kept the focus on the fields specifically dealt with. It has always been my practice to be as informal in my workshops as possible, encouraging questions at any time, and injecting humor at any opportunity. I have long regarded the art of cataloging to be a purposeful game of sorts, the object of which was to create an accurate, concise, useful, and informative bibliographic record. And, as far as I am concerned, it should usually be fun, if it is being done well.

Although the Playaway GMD debate may have been an extreme example, the exchanges that take place every day on cataloging discussion lists and that are reflected in cataloging question-and-answer columns regularly point up the topics that catalogers need to know more about. Some useful discussion lists or sources, followed by the Web addresses that explain how to subscribe, include the following:

- Online Audiovisual Catalogers' OLAC-List (http://www.olacinc.org/drupal/?q=node/51)

- Music OCLC Users Group's MOUG-L (http://www.musicoclcusers.org/listserv.html)

- Map cataloging and related lists (http://www.ala.org/ala/mgrps/rts/magert/help/askmap.cfm)

- OCLC-CAT and other OCLC lists (https:/www3.oclc.org/app/listserv)

Any creator of potentially useful workshops can take cues from such sources about the common cataloging problems of the day. And any cataloger trying to keep up with the rapidly changing twenty-first-century would do well to pay attention to these places where theory and reality clash.

CHAPTER 5

The Janus Effect: On-the-Job Training of Twenty-First-Century Catalogers

Deborah Lee

In the current zeitgeist, catalogers have adopted Janus-like qualities in order to survive and flourish.[1] One head faces the established cataloging rules of the past, which are based on the near-obsolete card catalog. The other head looks forward: it can see new cataloging rules on the horizon and the consequences of changes to the theoretical backbone of cataloging. However, the body is firmly rooted in the present amidst structural changes in cataloging departments, changes in cataloging workflow, and new formats to catalog. This tripartite approach to cataloging inevitably is reflected in the training of twenty-first-century catalogers.

Although there are different sources of cataloging training—such as library schools, external training courses, and on-the-job training—this chapter focuses on on-the-job training and suggests points to consider when designing this training.[2] The main purpose of training is to bring about a change (Creth 1986, 3): an employee may acquire a new skill or refine an existing one.[3] Moreover, the standard of their work is directly related to their training (Creth 1986, 1). Applying this to cataloging, on-the-job training is the guardian of the quality of the library's catalog.

On-the-job training is needed in various scenarios and takes on a number of different guises.[4] Each institution has its own unique, evolving needs that will require ongoing staff training. New employees, even when they are experienced catalogers, undoubtedly will need to learn about local cataloging rules, work flow, and possibly the library management system. A new job might also involve cataloging new types of material. On-the-job training is particularly vital for recent library school graduates as they face additional issues concerning the quantity, depth, and practical application of their cataloging education.[5] Finally, not everyone needing cataloging training will be a professional librarian: on-the-job training is also required for paraprofessionals who perform cataloging tasks.[6]

Considering ideas from education theory and from instructional design theory in particular can help when establishing a new cataloging training programme or modifying a preexisting one. One such instructional design model is ADDIE, which divides the process of organizing training into analysis, design, development, implementation, and evaluation stages (Molenda 2004, 7).[7] The first two stages of the ADDIE model—analysis and design—are particularly useful when applied to cataloging training, and ideas from these stages form the basis of this chapter.

This chapter first considers the overall contents of the cataloging training.[8] This is followed by a section outlining ideas about the organizational structure of the training. Next, possible training delivery methods are discussed, and their potential application to cataloging training is explored. Assessment and documentation are also briefly discussed. Practicalities such as the timing and location of training sessions are then considered. The final part of the chapter highlights specific issues concerning the rationale behind cataloging and the cataloging rules and the importance of imparting these to trainees. The general points in this chapter are occasionally highlighted with examples from the author's own experiences, devising a cataloging training program at the Courtauld Institute of Art, London.[9] This chapter draws attention to the particular challenges of cataloging training in the twenty-first century, where cataloging rules devised for the twentieth century are frequently taught to "children" of the twenty-first.

THE "WHAT": WHAT SHOULD BE INCLUDED IN THE TRAINING?

The objectives of the training should be the first consideration. Objectives will center around the type of material the trainees will be working with and the cataloging level that is expected and are ascertained from the trainee's job description. For instance, some trainees may work only with printed materials; others may catalog printed, electronic, and moving-image materials as part of their role. Similarly, trainees may be required to create basic, descriptive records only, or they may be required to perform high-level cataloging in both descriptive and subject cataloging, including classification. All these aspects need to be accounted for when designing the training.

In addition, the existing knowledge and background of each trainee should also inform the design of the training. At the macrolevel, information about whether a trainee has been previously employed as a cataloger is important; similarly, whether the trainee has been to library school is also important for the design of training. On a microlevel, more details about these experiences are needed, such as the level of cataloging they performed in previous employments and the depth of their cataloging experience at library school. This is particularly important when considering cataloging training in the twenty-first century. As previously noted in this chapter (see note 5), commentators have witnessed a decrease in the amount of time devoted to traditional cataloging in present-day library schools, and the effects of this must be factored in designing cataloging training. However, cataloging and activities allied to cataloging have become increasingly democratized in the twenty-first-century workplace, where these tasks are now performed by many different departments; this means that new employees from all library backgrounds are likely to be familiar with a Machine-Readable Cataloging 21 (MARC21) record from activities such as downloading records.[10]

Points to consider are the following:

- What are the formats of the materials the trainees will be expected to catalog after their training?
- Does the trainee have any specialized subject knowledge that could be useful for cataloging, such as a background in geography for map cataloging?
- Consider the level of cataloging expected of a trainee. For instance, will they be creating full-level records or less complete ones?
- How much of the record will trainees be expected to catalog? Will they be doing subject cataloging, doing authority work, and/or assigning classification numbers?
- What cataloging experience does trainees bring to their positions? Did they do any original cataloging and/or copy cataloging in their previous employments? If they have cataloging experience, how confident are they, and would they value some revision sessions?
- Has the trainee been to library school, and, if so, how much cataloging did they cover? Did they get any practical experience, or was is it purely theoretical?

THE "HOW": THE ORDER AND ORGANIZATION OF TRAINING

Once the aims of the cataloging training have been fixed, the order and organization of the training must be considered. An important part of this process is creating the intended progression through different types of catalog record. Traditionally, writers of cataloging training advice (e.g., Hudson 1987; Fitzgerald 1989) outline a training scheme where records that require the least editing are tackled first. From here, trainees then encounter more complex cataloging and editing until the apex is reached: original cataloging. Theoretically, this approach works on the assumption that the level of knowledge needed increases with the amount of content supplied by the trainee.

However, there is another approach. At the Courtauld, editing a downloaded record is considered to require a careful and judicious knowledge of cataloging rules as well as a good helping of knowledge of local practice in order to adapt these records for local use.[11] It is easier to create something fresh than to have the knowledge and confidence to edit someone else's work—whether editing out mistakes or adapting to local practice. Therefore, the Courtauld cataloging training program starts with original cataloging and only later considers downloaded records. An informal study from the 2008–2009 cohort at the Courtauld revealed many more cases of required alterations not being performed in downloaded records than mistakes in original records.

Another approach to organizing training is to center the training program on unchecked or lightly checked "stock," dealing with issues as they come up. Holley (2002, 49) describes this more serendipitous method when teaching cataloging at a library school. He claims that a randomly selected group of items uncovers real-life problems, which sparks interesting discussions; these are invaluable to learning real-life cataloging. However, Holley did concede that this method might cause certain key points to be missed erroneously from training. This raises a question concerning the treatment of difficult materials in cataloging training and at what point trainees encounter it. The purpose of on-the-job cataloging training is to prepare trainees for real items that come with real issues; however, trainees need to gain confidence in fundamental tasks, such as transcription, capitalization, and knowledge of subfields, before they can hope to get to grips with more challenging material—however prolific that material is within a cataloging section.

The order in which different types of materials are presented must also be considered in situations where a member of staff will catalog different formats of material as part of their role. Intner (2002, 21–23) outlines two different approaches in the library school setting, and these can be applied equally to on-the-job training. One is that all formats are taught throughout the training; the other is that a basic format, such as books, is taught first, with other formats added once trainees are familiar with the basic format. Cataloging all formats throughout training reflects the collections of a twenty-first-century library and the general trend for contents to transcend its format; however, focusing on the familiar book format allows trainees to fully understand the theory of cataloging before they meet other formats (Arsenault and Leide 2003, 194–96).

Points to consider are the following:

- Think about the organization of cataloging training at the beginning of your training design process.
- Determine which cataloging level is the most complex in your library and design your training to work towards that level in steps and stages.
- If you need to train catalogers in different types of formats, decide whether all formats should be taught at once or whether nonbook formats should be introduced as a separate topic later in the training. See Arsenault and Leide (2003) for a theoretical introduction to this debate.

THE "HOW": TRAINING DELIVERY METHODS, ASSESSMENT, AND DOCUMENTATION

Creth (1986, 44–47) discusses various different methods used for library training, and a number of these will be familiar to catalogers and cataloging trainers. Creth states that the demonstration method is the most frequently used by librarians (1986, 44). This method is useful for teaching skills within a trainee's actual workplace. For example, this is valuable for training someone how to complete a task using a particular library management system. The lecture method imparts large quantities of background or technical knowledge to a number of people at once; therefore, learning will take on a passive guise (Creth 1986, 45). For example, this method is useful for providing basic theoretical knowledge about the second edition of the *Anglo-American Cataloguing Rules* (AACR2) and the MARC21 format for trainees without this background. However, as Creth (1986, 45) states, the passive nature of this method is a disadvantage, and therefore it is better if it is used in conjunction with other methods. The discussion method gives trainees an opportunity to talk through ideas both in a formal and an informal method. This can have great value in cataloging training in the workplace; for instance, discussions about difficult-to-catalog items can reinforce the idea that cataloging is a cerebral and analytical activity.

Reviewing a trainee's work and progress has traditionally been part of cataloging training (see, e.g., Hudson 1987, 722; Fitzgerald 1991, 111) and is just as vital in the twenty-first-century library. Reviewing a trainee's work has two main purposes. The first purpose is to provide information about the trainee's understanding of cataloging and draws attention to any issues. This information is then reflected by the trainer; for instance, they might repeat key concepts in future training sessions or provide individual support. The second purpose of reviewing work is to determine whether a trainee has reached an appropriate standard to work independently or to progress to more demanding cataloging. In education theory terms, reviewing work for the first purpose is called formative assessment and, for the second, summative assessment (Haydn 2001, 289).

It is useful for assessment to take place at various stages both during and after the cataloging training. At the Courtauld, there are three complementary reviewing activities: informally checking trainees' work during training sessions, either by asking for answers to a class exercise or by discussing work with individuals during practice sessions; asking for written answers to between-session exercises, where more formal comments and corrections can be offered; and, after the end of the training course until an appropriate juncture, providing corrections and feedback for each cataloged item. Although most assessment during cataloging training is formative—the trainer is interested in how to adapt the training to address issues in trainees' work—the posttraining session assessment takes on some summative aspects. This period of time, often called the review or revision period, will be used to determine if and when the trainee becomes a fully fledged cataloger.[12]

The use of documentation is an important consideration when planning cataloging training. A formal training course may make use of a training manual that is prepared in advance by the trainer. The advantage of a training manual is that it can be reused each time the training takes place; the disadvantage is the time it takes to create a manual in the first place. In addition, specially prepared handouts or copies of salient pages from cataloging books or websites may be used to enhance cataloging training. These are particularly useful where there is a lot of pertinent detailed information to copy from a presentation or to transcribe from oral delivery.[13]

Training manuals are not the only useful documentation: if the library has standard documentation or manuals for its regular catalogers, then these can also be utilized. For example, it may be appropriate to ask trainees to read certain sections of a standard cataloging manual between training sessions. Ensuring that documentation is accurate and up to date is a vital part of preparing cataloging training; confusion created by finding differences between the cataloging manual and the training sessions is detrimental to the learning process. Finally, it is important that the usefulness of the library's cataloging documentation is embedded within the training sessions so that trainees refer to the documentation even when they have metamorphosed into fully fledged catalogers.

Points to consider are the following:

- If you are running a multiple-session cataloging training course, different methods will be useful for different parts of the training. For instance, consider a lecture-style method for the history and purpose of cataloging and a demonstration method for inputting diacritics into the cataloging module of the library management system.

- In the lecture parts of the training, consider using open questions, discussions, or small worksheets so that sessions include some active learning.

- Vary the learning styles where possible, especially in longer training sessions.

- Think about how you will assess the trainees' work and how you will use the information garnered from the assessment to address issues.

- Consider what training documentation will be provided. Check that any existing manuals or guidelines are accurate and up to date.

THE "WHERE" AND THE "WHEN": THE PRACTICALITIES OF TRAINING

Designing a cataloging training program is similar to designing any training program: practicalities of timings and training space must be considered at the outset. The total training time must be sufficient to cover all the required material. However, it must also take into account the total available time that can be devoted to the program by trainees and also the trainers. Once the total training time has been determined, the frequency and duration of sessions must be determined. The training timetable will depend on the schedules of trainees and trainers, but it must also take into account the time required to absorb knowledge and to practice. For example, the first year that a formal cataloging program was run at the Courtauld, sessions were run twice a week for two weeks. As the trainees had many other tasks to do apart from cataloging, this gave them very little time to absorb information between sessions or to practice. The next year, the sessions ran once a week: this problem was then alleviated.

Keeping sessions reasonably short is also important. Creth (1986, 71) claims that if a subject is technical, a trainee will be able to concentrate fully for only 30 or 40 minutes. The timing of sessions can also have an impact on the knowledge absorbed: different people work best at different times of day and on different days of the week.

The training location is a significant factor, and locating suitable training spaces is usually the cataloging trainer's responsibility. One possibility is the trainee's regular workstation. Advantages include the easy access to all relevant computer software, documents, and relevant paraphernalia; disadvantages include the presence of distractions for the trainee and interruptions from staff members or readers. However, there are times when training at the workstation is the most appropriate venue: for instance, real-life demonstrations of the library management system can be successfully carried out at a trainee's desk as well as cataloging demonstrations using the library's real-life work flow.

A different space is advisable for other parts of the cataloging training, and potential venues will depend on the organization. When considering training spaces, an important consideration is the availability of networked computers and whether specialist software such as the library management system will be needed. Another consideration is the working environment; for instance, training can be disrupted by insufficient light, excess heat, or external noise. In some circumstances, the distance and route between library and training room become significant, such as when many heavy books are needed for demonstration or practice. Usually, the perfect training space does not exist; compromise is crucial.[14]

Points to consider are the following:

- Calculate a realistic total training time based on the topics that need to be covered and the availability of trainers and trainees.
- It often takes more time to teach a task than anticipated, so build extra time into the schedule to take account of this.
- Think about the most effective frequency of training sessions.
- Consider which times of day are best times for training.
- Avoid making individual sessions too long and aim to distribute more difficult ideas across multiple sessions.
- Consider the training location as early in the design process as possible in order to source and secure the most ideal rooms. In some institutions, training rooms get booked up quickly.

- Visit the training room and test the computers before the training session itself. This will help avoid problems and technical delays during training.

- Generally, some compromises may have to be made over the amount of training time and/or the learning environment. Knowing about the significance of these compromises in advance should reduce their impact.

THE "WHY": REASONS TO CATALOG AND THE RATIONALE BEHIND CATALOGING RULES

This chapter started by asking why workplace cataloging training was needed. This has come full circle as we return to the question of "why": it will be argued that the "whys" of cataloging are an important part of the training process, and ways to encourage trainees to consider the reasons for what they are doing will be suggested.

As mentioned in the opening of this chapter, the process of cataloging can be modeled in two different ways: a mechanical process bound to a set of predetermined rules or a cerebral task requiring the use of discretion or interpretation. Naturally, the reality usually lies somewhere in between. In order for cataloging to approach the latter, the reasons behind cataloging and cataloging rules must entwine with training in the practicalities of training. Following Reece's (Luther Henderson 1987, 7) designation, this is where training becomes education.[15]

There are practical ways to ensure the reasons for cataloging become part of cataloging training, for example, as part of the introduction to the training. At the Courtauld, trainees were asked to think about the reasons for cataloging as a discussion point in the first training session. One of the most important purposes of cataloging should arise from such a discussion and arguably should be emphasized to trainees at every stage of the cataloging training process: retrieval. Without cataloging or with substandard cataloging, readers are disadvantaged when seeking the items they need.

Part of the process of retrieval is the method that mediates the cataloger's information to the reader, namely, the Online Public Access Catalog (OPAC). Whether used directly by readers or through the medium of a reference librarian, the OPAC is undoubtedly the public face of the cataloger's work in making items retrievable. Lee Hoerman (2002, 34–35) comments that one of the main communication problems between catalogers and reference librarians is that catalogers rarely use their own OPACs. Asking trainees to examine their records on the OPAC—such as looking at records display, browse searching, and key word searching—as part of their training should help bridge this gap between retrieval and cataloging.

Another reason to emphasize retrieval when training catalogers is that it provides one explanation for the obligatory attention to detail involved in cataloging. As Attar (2006, 181) emphasized in her article on a student cataloger project, if those expected to catalog do not understand the purpose of what they are doing, the consequences of shoddy spelling or incorrect nonfiling characters will not be realized. Linking attention to detail with retrieval will help those learning to catalog to understand one reason why it is so important.

Training catalogers to use AACR2 in the twenty-first century brings its own unique set of challenges. AACR2 was designed for a world where browsing was the main method of catalog retrieval and it was time consuming to produce information on a catalog card; it is a trainer's challenge to teach AACR2 in the very different context of today's online catalogs.[16] Issues arise when teaching rules that make little sense within a twenty-first-century library but were pertinent within the library environment that AACR2 was created for. Examples include selecting the main entry or understanding the "rule of three." There are great benefits to cataloging training when the origins and original purpose of such outmoded rules are explained.

Taking this one step further, a possible hypothesis is that training catalogers in the twenty-first-century requires a reimagination of the card catalog in order to fully understand and learn the rules of cataloging. One particular challenge of cataloging training in the twenty-first century is the disjuncture between twentieth-century cataloging rules and the twenty-first-century information retrieval background of the majority of the trainees. Put simply, trainees who were students themselves in the twenty-first century will not have encountered information retrieval in the same way as those who studied earlier.

There are two types of cataloging rules where this is particularly true. The first are cataloging rules related to indexing and indexes. The search environment has changed dramatically in the past few decades. The importance of the browse index has been superseded by key word searching (Antelman, Lynema, and Pace 2006, 128), meaning that rules such as nonfiling indicators and added title entries for parallel titles or portions of titles become less instinctive. In addition, whole concepts, such as the differentiation between main entries and added entries, are unfathomable if your only experience of retrieval is through online catalogs. Nevertheless, trainees must still learn to use these rules correctly.[17] One solution is that twenty-first-century catalog training re-creates the information retrieval zeitgeist that underpins the tenets of the cataloging rules. Card catalogs and browsing must be conjured up in the twenty-first-century cataloging training classroom.

Points to consider are the following:

- Discuss the reasons for cataloging as part of the training.
- Relate cataloging rules and concepts to effective retrieval of items by readers.

- Consider viewing catalog records on the OPAC as part of the training process.
- Reimagine or use a real card catalog during the training, particularly for explaining concepts such as browsing and main entry and added entries.

CONCLUSION

This chapter has considered some of the concepts and ideas important to designing cataloging training in the twenty-first-century library. Determining the objectives of the training should always be the first step, and these objectives will inform the whole planning process. While some training ideas are as important now as they were 20 years ago, the twenty-first-century library brings new challenges. For instance, the changes in library school curricula mean that traditional assumptions about a new graduate's cataloging skills must be discarded. However, twenty-first-century cataloging training is not just situated in the present and future; to fully understand present-day cataloging and cataloging rules, trainees need to understand past practices of retrieval and to reimagine its card catalog roots. Therefore, twenty-first-century libraries need an army of Janus-like catalogers where each one trains their recruits to look to the past, present, and future.

NOTES

1. The author would like to thank Dr. Julian Gilbey and Derek Lee for their help and guidance in producing this chapter and Antony Hopkins, Kilfinan Librarian at the Courtauld Institute of Art, for his support.
2. The necessary bridge between library school and day-to-day cataloging in the workplace is most likely to be provided by on-the-job training in the United Kingdom. External cataloging events do not usually provide practical training—aside from the subject or form-specific courses provided by specialist library organizations such as ARLIS, IAML, and the CILIP Rare Books and Special Collections group—and the basic courses provided by CILIP are too short to be a cataloger's only source of training (Bowman 2006, 324–26).
3. One long-standing issue in cataloguing literature is the conflict between cataloging training and cataloging education. In 1936, Ernst J. Reece wrote (Luther Henderson 1987, 7) that cataloging training is traditionally understood to involve repetitive tasks, with a schism between cataloging and the meaning of cataloging; however, he considers cataloging education to be a cerebral activity that involves analysis and the employment of discretion. This distinction is fundamental to how catalogers perceive themselves and their work. In these terms, this chapter concerns itself with cataloging education in the workplace, as I argue that context and thought are essential requirements for cataloging. However, the term "training" is adopted, as this term fits more comfortably in the workplace setting. In addition, "trainees" is used to describe those receiving instruction in cataloging in the workplace.

4. One recent survey demonstrates the need for training by taking recent library school graduates as its population. Mugridge (2008, 70–71) surveyed cataloging librarians. She found that 92 percent of her respondents had required some form of training when commencing their positions; this took the form of on-the-job cataloging training or external courses.

5. When Bowman (2004, 311–21) surveyed the cataloging education on offer at library schools in the United Kingdom, he found that most schools devote little time to cataloging and few offer practical training. Bowman (2004, 310) suggests that the infamous decrease in cataloging education in America has also been replicated in the United Kingdom. Whalen Moss (2007) summarizes her interviews with library school staff concerning the provision of cataloging and classification training in the United Kingdom. She discovered that though there was demand for cataloging and classification from students, there were many factors that indicate a progressive decrease in curriculum time devoted to these areas.

6. Paraprofessional staff include graduate trainees. Graduate trainees are library employees, usually employed on a yearlong program. They have not yet attended library school and are usually participating in the graduate trainee programme both to find out whether library work is suitable for them and to fulfill the employment prerequisite of British library schools. Graduate trainees perform a mixture of library assistant tasks coupled with a strong training ethos and are often given many opportunities for library visits and other forms of professional development.

7. More precisely, ADDIE is a set of models sharing common characteristics (Molenda 2004, 7).

8. It should be pointed out that my experience is with cataloging training in the United Kingdom. Although this chapter is not specifically about organizing training in the United Kingdom, it will inevitably reflect this bias.

9. Although the author is responsible for all in-house cataloging training, the majority of training is for each year's intake of graduate trainees. Graduate trainees perform paraprofessional-level cataloging throughout their tenure and are trained to do original cataloging and edit downloaded records as part of their yearlong training program. A formal cataloging training program was introduced in October 2008 to replace the ad hoc cataloging training offered to previous graduate trainees.

10. Complications arise when two or more new members of staff need training and they have different cataloging backgrounds. This phenomenon occurred at the Courtauld, when a library school graduate started as a library assistant at a similar time to the graduate trainees. After a discussion with the library assistant to assess their previous knowledge, it was decided that they would attend the final two sessions of the graduate trainee cataloging course in order to gain specific skills knowledge, such as cataloging art materials and learning local Courtauld cataloging policies.

11. Over half the Courtauld's cataloging backlog—from which the graduate trainees learn to catalog—consists of exhibition catalogs. Finding high-quality, downloaded records for these items is relatively rare; the records

that are found are often brief or follow non-AACR2 cataloging rules, making much work for the cataloger.

12. In recent years, there has been much research on the pedagogical bene-fits of formative assessment—for example, see Black and Williams (1998) and its successors.

13. When considering the contents of the training, trainers must also consider the use of formal documentation, such as AACR2 and the MARC21 manuals, and how trainees will be taught to use these sources for themselves.

14. At the Courtauld, it is traditional for staff training to be carried out at the staff member's desk, but this was found wanting for cataloging training. Therefore, most cataloging training is carried out in one of the institute's general seminar rooms. This provides an interruption-free environment for cataloging training. Although there are disadvantages—for instance, lack of access to the library management system—the overall benefits are deemed to outweigh these.

15. The cause and effect could be considered the other way around: precisely because we need all these things included, cataloging can be designated a cerebral activity.

16. Antelman, Lynema, and Pace (2006, 128) outline the history of OPACs and the search methods used to retrieve information at different points in time.

17. As discussed by Howarth and Weihs (2008, 217), the "rule of three" has been abolished in Resource Description and Access (RDA); however, though "main entry" and "added entry" are due to change their titles in RDA, the concepts look set to continue (Howarth and Weihs 2008, 217).

REFERENCES

Antelman, Kristen, Emily Lynema, and Andrew K. Pace. "Toward a Twenty-First Century Library Catalog." *Information Technology & Libraries* 25 (2006): 128–39.

Arsenault, Clément, and John E. Leide. "Format Integration and the Design of Cataloging and Classification Curricula." In*Education for Cataloging and the Organization of Information: Pitfalls and the Pendulum*, ed. Janet Swan Hill, 189–202. New York: Haworth, 2003.

Attar, K. E. "Why Appoint Professionals? A Student Cataloguing Project." *Journal of Librarianship and Information Science* 38 (2006): 173–85.

Black, Paul, and Dylan Williams. *Inside the Black Box: Raising Standards through Classroom Assessment.* London: King's College London, 1998.

Bowman, J. H. "Education and Training for Cataloguing and Classification in the British Isles." *Cataloging & Classification Quarterly* 41 (2006): 309–33.

Creth, Sheila. *Effective on the job training.* Chicago: American Library Association, 1986.

Fitzgerald, Michael. "Training the Cataloger: A Harvard Experience." In *Recruiting, Educating, and Training Cataloging Librarians: Solving the*

Problems, ed. Shelia S. Intner and Janet Swan Hill, 341–53. New York: Greenwood, 1989.

Haydn, Terry. "Assessment and Accountability." In *Learning to Teach in the Secondary School: A Companion to School Experience*, ed. Susan Capel, Marilyn Leask, and Tony Turner, 287–312. London: RoutledgeFalmer, 2001.

Holley, Robert P. "Cataloguing: An Exciting Subject for Exciting Times." In *Education for Cataloging and the Organization of Information: Pitfalls and the Pendulum*, ed. Janet Swan Hill, 43–52. New York: Haworth, 2002.

Howarth, Lynne C., and Jean Weihs. "Enigma Variations: Parsing the Riddle of Main Entry and the "Rule of Three" from AACR2 to RDA." *Cataloging & Classification Quarterly* 46 (2008): 201–20.

Hudson, Judith. "On-the-Job Training for Cataloging and Classification." *Cataloging & Classification Quarterly* 7 (1987): 69–78.

Intner, Sheila S. "Persistent Issues in Cataloging Education: Considering the Past and Looking toward the Future." In *Education for Cataloging and the Organization of Information: Pitfalls and the Pendulum*, ed. Janet Swan Hill, 15–30. New York: Haworth, 2002.

Lee Hoerman, Heidi. "Why Does Everybody Hate Cataloging?" In *Education for Cataloging and the Organization of Information: Pitfalls and the Pendulum*, ed. Janet Swan Hill, 31–41. New York: Haworth, 2002.

Luther Henderson, Kathryn. "Some Persistent Issues in the Education of Catalogers and Classifiers." *Cataloging & Classification Quarterly* 7 (1987): 5–26.

Molenda, Michael. "The ADDIE Model." In *Education and Technology: An Encyclopedia*, ed. Ann Kovalchik and Kara Dawson, 7–10. Santa Barbara, CA: ABC-CLIO, 2004.

Mugridge, Rebecca. "Experiences of Newly-Graduated Cataloging Librarians." *Cataloging & Classification Quarterly* 45 (2008): 61–79.

Whalen Moss, Kathleen. "Swings and Roundabouts: The Role of Cataloguing and Classification in the LIS Curriculum." *Catalogue & Index*, no. 155 (2007): 2–5.

CHAPTER 6

Managing Vendor Cataloging to Maximize Access

Rebecca L. Lubas

Outsourcing. The "O" word. It conjures up images of overseas call centers. The mere whisper of it inspires attacks of job security anxiety. In the general economic climate of recent years and the decline of staff numbers in technical services, such reactions are understandable.

Some of these concerns are well founded, as outsourcing has been used for replacing salaried, full-time staff in libraries. But it does not need to be this way. Outsourcing is a tool in the catalog manager's toolbox and, used well, can help achieve effective results. The best tools save your energy and strength for more important work. Outsourcing can serve this purpose.

Outsourcing has helped many libraries, offering quick turnaround and helping us juggle increasing and expanding responsibilities (Stump 2006, 30). In our world of instant access, fast delivery is important and ever more challenging as information proliferates. Quality and quantity are always in tension (Stump 2006, 31).

In this chapter, I examine the range of outsourcing options available and how the catalog manager can make the most of available products and services and how to approach preparing for outsourcing. Outsourcing should be not a last resort but rather an option used to consider using to maximize the resources you have and use your precious human resources most wisely.

With strategy and planning, outsourcing choices can improve service (Bierman 2008, 49). In this chapter, I examine how to make sound decisions about vendor cataloging products. The chapter looks at the factors to consider regarding why outsourcing might be a good choice in many situations, what types of vendor cataloging products are available, and how some products can add useful metadata to your catalog that you would not be able to manage manually. It also looks at how to investigate the impacts implementing outsourced cataloging on your local work flows and how to begin, test, and assess the process. Incorporating vendor products can enhance the metadata in your local catalog if choices based on your library's needs and human resources are carefully considered.

GETTING STARTED

The first, most important question: why? Many libraries turn to outsourcing cataloging as a band-aid. They have built up a large backlog, are unable to fill a vacancy (or vacancies), or have material that requires expertise that they cannot access easily, such as familiarity with a non-Roman language or a special format. All these are situations that outsourcing can address. But such crises are not the only situations that prompt outsourcing, and considering what outsourcing can do during a nonemergency time can be of great benefit. Approach outsourcing as you would face shopping for a second car before the first one breaks down. You will make better decisions if you do them strategically and not while under pressure to make a quick decision.

Since many of us face smaller staff numbers, taking stock of the skill set you have in-house is a must, even if you are not considering hiring a vendor or buying cataloging records. It is easy to take for granted that you know the capabilities of your staff—but do you remember who took an online workshop in electronic resource cataloging with their professional development award last year? Do you know off the top of your head who in your library has which language skills? "In-source" first.

Knowing the library's priorities is the key to planning:

- Is your library pursuing an aggressive policy of purchasing electronic formats when available instead of print?
- What digitization projects is your library involved in?
- What projects do you as a catalog manager want your staff to be involved in but maybe you are not because you are too busy with the books that have not disappeared yet?

One answer to "Why outsource?" may be because you want to use your valuable human resources in a way other than their current deployment.

But What about Those Crisis Situations?

You are short staffed, in a hiring freeze, with a growing backlog. A large gift has been made to the library of material in a non-Roman language that no one on staff can read or a format no one in your department has experience cataloging. Although in these cases seeking a vendor or outside contractor to fill your needs may be a one-time solution, the project should still be approached with strategy and planning.

The first question should be if the one-time situation is truly one time. The University of New Mexico had a large gift of sound recordings on compact discs—over 5,000 titles. While there were trained music catalogers, the volume of the gift plus current receipts would have taken years to complete. Hiring a vendor to catalog the items for us was heavily considered; however, it was a given that other music gifts were sought by collection development. A more sustainable long-term solution was to increase the number of catalogers who could work with music material. The training investment was worth it, knowing that this one-time situation would likely recur.

What Is Available?

A wide range of cataloging products and services are available from different providers. Products range from prepackaged record sets to individual contract catalogers for hire who will customize work to your exact specifications.

Languages

One of the most commonly accepted reasons for opting to outsource cataloging is lack of language expertise, especially for materials in languages using non-Roman alphabets. Services for languages that are in increasing demand are becoming easier to find. Catalog records in Spanish, in particular, are increasingly available (Alpert 2006, 95).

Vendors are often reluctant to put their reputation behind foreign language cataloging if they are unable to find an experienced cataloger for hire. The search becomes more difficult if you need special language and a special format. If you have a world music collection to catalog, for example, you may have to compromise and have a language expert and format expert work together.

Since language expertise is at a premium, purchasing cataloging for it will cost and will not necessarily be cheaper than completing the cataloging in-house. If you have very small yearly amounts of foreign languages that you can cumulate and batch or one-time gifts, outsourcing may be the most efficient way to deal with the material if you can find a vendor who will provide the given language. Contracting with an individual may be an option as well, especially if you can find someone who would like part-time occasional work, such as a retired cataloger.

Another approach to this type of material when your regular staff lack the expertise is to hire temporary project staff. Sometimes one can negotiate the use of student funds in an institution for temporary staff at a higher cost (of course, the budget is spent much more quickly this way). Term contracts offer the flexibility of hiring for a targeted skill without a long-term commitment.

Hiring contract staff for one or two years can improve the consistency of the work, as they would be locally trained (Leibowitz and Arthur 2008, 259). Also keep in mind that you do not have control over the turnover factor from a cataloging vendor.

If hiring temporary staff or contract staff is not possible and a vendor offering the necessary language skill is not found, look within. Your regular cataloging staff may not have the skills, but coupled with a student or someone else on the library staff, you may be able to accomplish your needs. In addition, examine your assumptions about who does what kind of tasks in your organization. Original cataloging by paraprofessionals is increasingly common (Ivey 2009, 464). This need not be a signal of decreased quality in cataloging. Often, paraprofessional, support staff catalogers or nondegreed catalogers have more direct cataloging experience than the professionals in a library and have seen trends in cataloging more quickly and in higher volume than the professionals. Increasingly, professional/degreed catalogers are charged with more management-type activities and see less cataloging. So, if you have a paraprofessional with language expertise, seriously consider assigning them the cataloging.

Shelf-Ready Services

Shelf-ready services are a popular first step into outsourcing for many cataloging departments. These services can do double duty by piggybacking services with a vendor providing book orders. The books come to the library with labels and security devices, and records are loaded during or after shipping.

One reason that shelf-ready is a payoff is the turnaround time. Coupled with the fact that many of the books from a book vendor have Library of Congress or Program for Cooperative Cataloging (PCC) copy, a library is not giving up the handling of unique or special items with this option.

Shelf-ready services often have leveled options beyond providing Library of Congress copy. For a charge, they will enhance less-than-full records.

Value-Added Services

A number of vendors provide enhanced data for your catalog in addition to new title cataloging. Vendors for authority work have been in operation since the early 1990s, and there are several large vendors providing this service as well as smaller vendors.

Outsourcing maintenance of the authority file without abdicating local control is possible. Your catalogers can continue to perform authority control on original records or records that they are enhancing and work in the national authority file if you are a participant in the Name Authority Cooperative

Program of the PCC. But the vendor can provide updates to records on a periodic basis. Coupled with automated processes such as global change in your integrated library system (ILS), you can have an up-to-date authority file with decreased manual effort.

Bibliographic records are organic and can be updated too. You may download a record into your catalog one day, and the next day or week another library loads a contents note and updated URL. These value-added services are worth considering if they provide material for discovery for your users. Tables of contents can be especially helpful for conference proceedings, for example. Bibliographic update services work well coupled with shelf-ready services. If your shelf-ready vendor provides you with cataloging-in-publication cataloging, your bibliographic update vendor can provide you with the fuller record when available.

Records Sets and Subscriptions

Sets of bibliographic records come in two main forms. There are static sets of records for collections of works that are sold as a package by a vendor. Bibliographic utilities such as the Online Computer Library Center sell many sets of large microform collections, for example. Many vendors sell records with sets of electronic books and journals (sometimes included in the price or at additional cost).

Dynamic records sets are an option, usually as a subscription, for ongoing collections. Government documents and journal aggregator packages are examples. These can be an attractive option when you have an "instant backlog" with the purchase of a large package. Since aggregator packages switch titles in and out frequently, subscribing to a record service is a possible answer to the manual maintenance of the records. Find out if a record set includes updates. Will you receive enhanced records or fuller records as they become available if the initial record supplied is less than full?

Record sets are a solution for collections of material that are on your "to-do" list but you have not been able to work them into your regular work flow. Sometimes the per-record cost is a bargain—a few pennies a record—and sometimes not. You need to consider the hidden costs. Will these records require much massaging? When you add in the staff time required to process an inexpensive set of records, are you still saving time and money?

In situations when the per-record charge seems expensive, consider how much staff time it would cost you to pull the records from a utility even without much editing of the record. Alternatively, does buying a package of records make sense if you will need to inventory and create item records for each title, thus still handling each piece?

INVESTIGATE

Making the decision to outsource is only the first step. Outsourcing does not mean you have washed your hands of the work. As one cataloging vendor noted, "I sell a product, not management" (Deborah Silverman, personal communication, October 7, 2009).

Approach the setup for outsourcing as a project, with a team. You will need to solicit input from all in the library who handle a cataloging record: acquisitions, cataloging, systems, processing, and frontline Online Public Access Catalog (OPAC) searchers. Remember that the front catalogers and systems workers, those who do the work in your ILS every day, will know best where the snags might be in loading records from a new source into your system.

Planning will prevent errors and misinterpretation by the vendor and thus later labor (Turbanti 2007, 457). Read your potential vendor's specification documentation carefully. Will their process allow you to do everything you want to do? Have the project team look over the specifications as well. They will have the expertise to know where the process will break down and where the work-arounds for the quirks of your local system need to be addressed.

This is also the time to think about why you may be asking vendors to do certain things. Are you asking them to put in a particular note because "that's the way you've always done it?" Beware of this as a justification. Again, your project team will be valuable. Often there was a good reason for the exception or process that has been created and handed down. Sometimes the reason is still valid but sometimes not. The project team should be able to enlighten you, so you as a manager not only avoid unnecessary exceptions but also do not unwittingly drop a data element that a much-used search in your OPAC depends on.

Do remember that nonstandard cataloging takes more time, whether you are doing it in-house or paying a vendor extra to do it for you. What is the value? Could you be doing something more important? (Stump 2006, 31).

If you do ask for customized options, you will pay more. Make sure it is worth it. Does it support a special program? Does it support a particular special search in your OPAC? Can the same result be achieved by reindexing your ILS? Also remember that the more "nonstandard" customizations you ask for, the more the likelihood of error (Silverman 2009).

PILOT PROJECTS AND SCALING UP

When outsourcing for the first time for an ongoing service or when working with a vendor for the first time, a pilot project on a small scale is a good way to work out issues. Pick out a subset of what you would like to outsource.

When selecting your subset, try to make it representative. If you pick the "low-hanging" fruit, you might find that you are bogged down with problems as you try to scale up.

When starting to use a shelf-ready cataloging service, firm orders make a good first target (Bierman 2008, 53). Do not start with approval orders unless your library had already made the decision that approvals are not returned. Do not target a single subject area, as different subject areas present different issues. If you select only science, you might not see how the vendor deals with the intricacies of classics with uniform titles. Selecting art, you may miss how conference headings are handled. Remember, once you have purchased shelf-ready cataloging, you can no longer return approvals, so you will need to decide what your tolerance is for accepting books that you may have wanted to return (Bierman 2008, 63).

It is good practice to have a communication plan beyond technical services. There will be impacts in the catalog and for the public, and having all corners of the library aware of the project will create an avenue for feedback.

ASSESS AND REASSESS

When planning your outsourcing project, in addition to planning a pilot and scaling-up stage, build in ongoing assessment. This achieves two important objectives. The first, more obvious one is that you want to do quality checks on your product and services. The second is to establish boundaries. Staff need to have trust in the service, or they will want to check everything the vendor does, and essentially you will end up paying for the work twice. You can help address these concerns with clear quality control plans and transparency. After an initial pilot and scaling-up stage, for example, you may want to take a once-a-year sample (or more frequently) and make the results of the sample available to the staff. Your project plan should address who will be in charge of the project once it is routine—to name a "shepherd."

WHAT NOT TO OUTSOURCE

Outsourcing everything is not viable (Bierman 2008, 65). How do you decide what can and cannot be outsourced? If your project team identifies unique local data that must be created, you may have a task to keep at home. Vendors may charge a high price to replicate the work, and because they do not work in your environment, they may not easily understand how to apply the exception, and the task may have a high error rate as well as a high dollar price. Unique material is a target to keep in-house, although, depending on the expertise needed to process and analyze it, hiring temporary project staff may be required.

So, What Do You Do with All This Spare Time? Is It Worth It?

Outsourcing may not cost you much less in dollars than having in-house staff do the work. A University of Nevada–Las Vegas shelf-ready study found that the process cost only two dollars less a book than having in-house staff perform the work (Bierman 2008, 61).

There is more than the dollar cost to consider. In our world of proliferating information, opportunity costs are important. You may not be able to get new staff lines added to your department to create metadata for digital projects or to manage a next-generation catalog layer. But you may be able to outsource work that your staff is doing now because a vendor makes it available, and your existing staff can take on these new tasks—tasks that need the kind of expertise catalogers have developed over decades of experience organizing information.

CONCLUSION

Outsourcing cataloging activities should be approached with the same care and thought as any other project or work flow revision in the library. It is not an abdication of control over your local data. Managing outsourced products requires the same skills and expertise built up over cataloging careers to make good decisions about product quality and utility. Instead of making these decisions on a record-by-record basis, you are making them for larger categories of material. You are judging the work of the vendor with the same expertise as you would judge a cataloger in training. If executed successfully, you can then reap the rewards of your efforts by using your expertise for unique materials and new initiatives in the library. By using contract staff and vendor products, you can employ outsourcing to reengineer your workload.

REFERENCES

Alpert, Phyllis Sue. "Effect of Multiculturalism and Automation on Public Library Collection Development and Technical Services." *Public Library Quarterly* 25 (2006): 1–2, 91–103.

Bierman, Kenneth J., and Judith A. Carter. "Outsourcing Monograph Cataloging at the UNLV Libraries." *Technical Services Quarterly* 25 (2008): 49–65.

Ivey, Robert T. "Perceptions of the Future of Cataloging: Is the Sky Really Falling?" *Cataloging & Classification Quarterly* 47 (2009): 464–82.

Leibowitz, Faye R., and Michael A. Arthur. "Risky Business: Outsourcing Serials Cataloging." *The Serials Librarian* 54 (2008): 253–60.

Stump, Sheryl. "Keeping Your Plates Spinning: Technical Services Tasks from Delta State's Perspective." *Mississippi Libraries* 70 (2006): 2, 30–32.

Turbanti, Simona. "La bonifica del catalogo e controllo di qualita?" *Bollettino* 47 (2007): 4, 451–59.

CHAPTER 7

Collaborating with Other Library Departments

Sever Bordeianu and Rebecca L. Lubas

Collaboration is the lifeblood of a library. Libraries depend on everyone working toward the same goals to provide quality service. There are several facets to collaboration, but it is important that they are all subordinate to the final goal of making the organization successful. Collaboration requires good communication; coordination; a common understanding of each department's place in the hierarchy of the organization; a mutual understanding of each other's rules, procedures, and practices; and feedback. Different departments have different needs, and they will naturally emphasize those over others. It is important that the organization prevent turf battles and vested interests in order to minimize wasteful practices.

While catalogers have long been in the practice of collaborating among themselves, unfortunately, the stereotype persists that cataloging is the most isolated of library specialties. This image is mostly unfair, as catalogers have long supported requests and responded to the needs of the greater organization. However, this perception persists and must be altered. Active collaboration is a response to this problem. Metadata managers can seek collaboration opportunities to promote the abilities and utility of their departments rather than simply responding to requests.

Libraries, in general, are focused primarily on end users. Catalogers, unlike many of their colleagues within their organization, are in the challenging position of being a few steps removed from direct patron interaction. Catalogers need to heighten their awareness of the information needs of the end users and of the other library departments and use their expertise to provide metadata that best serve those needs. For the right or the wrong reasons, catalogers have the reputation of a slavish adherence to rules and a total disregard for the needs of the end users, even when these end users are not properly served. We must remember that catalogers can customize records with information that does not conform to the rules in order to address user needs. As end users have an increasing universe of search options and expectations, the need to be aware of their behaviors is paramount.

Working more closely with colleagues around the library is an avenue to understanding end user needs better.

Collaboration is complex and can be difficult. Different departments may use different terminologies, and what is easily comprehensible to a cataloger may not mean anything to a systems librarian or a reference librarian. Departments may also exhibit different internal cultures, some being more hierarchical and others more equal. Often, this is dictated by the type of work performed in a department. But to ensure good collaboration, there needs to be a clear indication of who makes the final decision and who breaks the deadlocks.

In the cataloging realm, collaboration traditionally revolves around the online catalog. With the exception of the actual library building, perhaps nothing represents the library better than its catalog, even with the addition of databases and other resources. The catalog is at the center of many library services, from the delivery of information to teaching to developing the library's collections as well as showcasing the library as virtual place. Each one of these constituencies has different needs, and the catalog needs to be versatile enough to satisfy them. Cataloging also has allegiance to a national (and increasingly international) constituency since the rules and practices are designed and implemented by various national organizations. This connection is important, as cataloging is increasingly becoming a cooperative effort among many libraries that contribute cataloging records to the national databases and vendor services.

Thus, collaboration can help catalogers move past the boundaries of their library's catalog. Well-crafted, user-centric metadata can now have utility beyond the borders of the local catalog. Metadata can be reworked and repackaged to meet the user needs of the moment. Collaboration with our colleagues across the library and the profession will help us better understand and anticipate these needs. Twenty-first-century cataloging managers should use collaboration as yet another option in their toolbox to make the skills and product of their departments essential to the organization.

COLLABORATING BEHIND THE SCENES

It is always easiest and most comfortable to collaborate with those most like you. To build collaboration skills, look first to technical services colleagues and other "behind-the-scenes" library units. Collaboration with units that, like cataloging, work only indirectly with patrons and that also rely on catalog records for their work, such as acquisitions, systems, and collection development, comes naturally and effortlessly. With these departments, there is already a common terminology and a natural understanding of the work cycles, and, to a large extent, each unit depends on the others in the performance of its work.

Acquisitions

The acquisitions department is usually the first and most obvious target of collaboration with cataloging. Acquisitions are also considered a technical service, and often cataloging and acquisitions are geographically placed close together in the library. Catalogers have been collaborating with their colleagues "across the aisle" for decades, moving materials across the supply chain to the shelves. In many libraries, the lines between acquisitions and cataloging are blurred by "cataloging-on-receipt" procedures, where technical services employees are cross trained and can perform both functions or parts of both functions. Acquisitions are also critical partners in setting up and maintaining shelf-ready cataloging operations, as the lines between the functions are not neatly separated.

Over the past decade, the packaging and containers of library resources have morphed almost constantly. Electronic resources may be sold as bundles, licensed annually, or sold with permanent access rights. With the increase in e-resources and e-book readers becoming increasingly popular, vendors do not peddle their wares in a consistent way. Despite the value of "content over carrier," the carrier still has a profound impact on cataloging. Collaborating closely with our colleagues in acquisitions will help catalogers be aware of these trends earlier. Cataloger involvement earlier in the acquisition process can also have benefits for setting up end user access to the material.

Information Technology/Systems Departments

Collaborating with your library's systems department is essential in running the online catalog and other access tools smoothly and efficiently. Communication with our systems colleagues results in knowing the limitations and strengths of the system and how metadata behave in the system. Information technology departments are also vital in providing the infrastructure for maintaining and delivering information. In some libraries, cataloging and systems operations are so intertwined that they report to the same manager.

"Techies" or, even more colloquially, "computer geeks" may be the one group in the library world that has an even stronger stereotype of isolation than catalogers. Many who consider themselves non–computer savvy dread making technical requests because they do not speak the jargon. Communication is the cornerstone of overcoming this perceived barrier. The more you work directly with systems, the more you understand the language, and the more you know how to ask for what you want.

Catalogers have a deep knowledge of the rich resource that Machine Readable Cataloging (MARC) metadata can be for our services. We need to look at the systems department as partners in the delivery of that service. Catalogers and systems librarians need to work very closely in designing the online catalog and making sure that all its functions are utilized to their full potential. Cooperation between cataloging and systems needs to occur in the in the following areas: access points and indexing; data integrity, maintenance, and backup; public display and delivery options; and, last but not least, the maintenance and support of the individual catalogers' computers and of cataloging tools in general.

Systems librarians need to be aware of the strengths and limitations of the MARC record, and catalogers need to have sound understanding of the power and limitations of the system. System limitations that affect the function of the catalog and cataloging include the overall system storage capacity; the processing speed; the system's ability to update records, whether in real time or time delayed; parameters that govern searching and refining capabilities; and, finally, display options. The display options, which translate MARC record data into a streamlined display, easily understood by users, can often be customized. Certain MARC fields can be forced to display higher on the screen, while others can be suppressed from public view. Both systems librarians and catalogers need to have a thorough understanding of these options and limitations. And, of course, this will later lead to collaboration and consultation with public services for the best customization of the data display.

Collection Development

Collection development varies in its place in the organizational tree from library to library. Although collection development librarians must engage in direct public contact and outreach activities, it is often considered to be a technical service as well and may be closely coupled with the acquisitions department.

Collection development relies on good metadata to know the library's holdings for selection, collection analysis, and statistics reporting. The relationship between cataloging and collection development can be strengthened and expanded beyond merely one providing data for the other. Here is an excellent opportunity for the catalog manager to engage in outreach. Collection analysis and statistics reporting can be enhanced by better knowledge of the metadata available. Volunteering to help with a necessary task can improve the utility of the results.

Collection development relies on quality cataloging records added in a timely manner to the catalog. This is probably the single biggest contribution that cataloging can provide for collection development. Catalogers can provide brief records for books that are on order and, once the books have arrived in the library, provide quick and efficient cataloging. Outside the system, a well-organized cataloging backlog can help collection development and other public services easily find books that are in process.

In its cooperation with collection development, cataloging needs to teach the relevant MARC fields of the bibliographic record in order to make it easy for collection development librarians to interpret the records. Online catalogs typically have local fields that are not part of MARC, such as cataloging date, status (temp record or cataloged record), and some date fields that can show when a record has been ordered and whether it has been received. Collection development librarians need to be well versed with these fields in order to avoid duplicate orders, unnecessary claiming, and other confusion. A thorough understanding of catalog records will also enable collection development librarians to conduct proper inventories for collection maintenance projects.

Conversely, catalogers need to be equally aware of the technical environment in which collection development takes place. First and foremost are the time schedules and constraints of collection development. Usually, budgets are allocated and need to be expended during a fiscal year. Typically, collection development will order books during the fall and early spring part of the year. This means that materials will be received more intensely immediately following these periods when the bulk of ordered materials arrive. Usually, the summer months are a slower period for collection development. This usually leads cataloging departments to focus on regular receipts during the year and on projects during the summer and early fall.

Another major area of collaboration between collection development and cataloging is the area of vendor records. Increasingly, vendors can provide MARC records especially for large sets of books, such as electronic book packages. Often collection development is aware of the availability of these records before cataloging is. The two units need to work together to identify the site where the records are available, login and password procedures for accessing the records, evaluating the records, and customizing them before importing them into the online catalog. Customization consists in adding desired local fields that identify the collection or the vendor, adding the proxy addresses to the database, and tailoring non-MARC fixed fields or order records to specify licensing information. Collection development also has a vested interest in the loading schedules for these records, as it is important to make the records available to the users as soon as they are paid for.

Finally, well-cataloged records enable collection development librarians to showcase the collections, to provide lists of newly acquired materials, or, conversely, to conduct in-depth analyses of discreet collection areas as well as statistics. Collection analysis is important for supporting departmental program reviews in academic libraries, and statistics are an important tool of the Association of Research Libraries. These activities provide useful data outside the catalog, thus supporting the overall mission of the library.

COLLEAGUES ON THE FRONT LINES

Understanding what the end user seeks is key to providing better metadata and discovery tools. As catalogers do not usually have much contact with the public, closer collaboration with our colleagues in direct contact services can help us reach a better understanding of our users. In this area more than any other, learning from each other is paramount. Too often catalogers are satisfied with providing good-quality cataloging but with no awareness of how that catalog record behaves or how it is used by the public. Uniform titles for foreign language books are only one example that baffles the public. Catalogers need to know how the public searches for books and journals, which fields are unnecessary or confusing, which fields are not used, and how the display options in the online catalog can be manipulated to make a more easily understandable record.

Reference

The provision of public services and especially of access to the library's content depends in great part on the online catalog. A good catalog, with quality records, is important for quality reference work. It is also important for public services staff to understand the catalog and the records.

An easy outreach opportunity is the offer of training. A catalog manager can offer to train new reference staff or provide refresher courses to "better know the catalog." Often, integrated library systems have searches available in the staff mode that can assist a reference librarian in especially tricky questions.

Knowing better the needs of reference librarians and the users they work with is critical to being able to judge one of the more time-consuming activities in cataloging: customization. Cataloging has a long tradition of adding information locally to create more effective searches, for example, by adding varying titles, department names, and other local information. Sometimes adding this information is a "work-around" for pitfalls of the local integrated library system. Customization should always be rigorously evaluated not only because it is labor intensive but also because as your data deviate from national records, loss of interoperability and migration headaches could await down the line. Customization often has unintended consequences. By better understanding how public services librarians are using the catalog, you can better evaluate which customizations are truly needed. It is also important to make sure that desired customization is not deleted when new records are brought in, for example, if a library subscribes to the "Bibliographic Update" service.

Catalogers are in the best position to advise public services staff which changes are realistic to make, such as adding an alternate title, adding local holdings information, cross-referencing a department's name, or customizing a URL and then making sure that the changes are protected in the system. Collaboration in this area can produce very beneficial results and greatly add to the value of the catalog.

Gregory, Weber, and Dippie (2008) mention that when Eccless library started experimenting with chat reference, it was partly staffed with technical services librarians. This was for two separate reasons. One was their expertise in information organization and analysis. The other was their proximity to and knowledge of the library's collection. As the ones in charge of ordering, receiving, and cataloging all the library's materials, these technical services librarians had firsthand knowledge of the latest materials available from the library (Gregory et al. 2008, 43).

User-Created Tags

User comments, or "tags," are now common throughout the Web. An initial reaction to this user-provided metadata may be that it is "messy" and "uncontrolled" and therefore not worth the trouble. However, users of common shopping sites expect this information and make use of it. Instead of viewing tags as "wild metadata," consider their value as access points. If you add a tagging system to your Online Public Access Catalog, you increase access points, and thus users have more paths to discover your library's collection (Steele 2009, 77). As with any public participation, there are downsides, such as a complete lack of authority control and, on a more ominous level, malicious tagging (Steele 2009, 71). Libraries can work around some of these problems by reviewing the tags both for appropriateness and for spelling. Exercise a small amount of quality control over user-submitted tags, and you can become a collaborator with the public itself.

Circulation, Interlibrary Loan, and Document Delivery

Access services depend on the catalog to be reliable. A poorly cataloged book is potentially a lost book. Interlibrary loan (ILL) and its extension, document delivery, depend strongly on quality and well-maintained records. Most libraries use the Online Computer Library Center ILL system or another service that is run on MARC records. There are two aspects in which ILL uses the catalog information for identification and delivery of the information. First, the correct and appropriate record for a book or journal needs to be in the catalog. Second, the proper holdings information needs to be in the ILL database (either WorldCat or another system). WorldCat is the domain of catalogers. Cataloging managers need to be aware and make sure that WorldCat holdings for all "lendable" materials, whether print or electronic, are reflected in WorldCat. Procedures for updating holdings and removing them, as materials are added or withdrawn, are essential. In some cases, libraries use other ILL systems that may need data extracted from the local online catalog. All this information is maintained at the item level by the cataloging department.

In either case, a good system depends on close collaboration between cataloging and ILL. It also has to be timely. For physical materials, if it is not in the catalog, it does not exist.

Instruction

Like reference, this department interfaces directly with the end users, and, like reference, this collaboration is a two-way street. Instruction is another group that could benefit from a "better-know-the-catalog" outreach activity. This interaction enables the library to find out what works and what does not. Instruction librarians need to familiarize themselves with the latest implementations in the catalog, the latest cataloging rules, and the current environment in which the cataloging department operates. They are in the best position to teach the primary users the latest techniques for the best search strategies. They can explain how to interpret data displayed in public records and how to contact the library when they have problems.

They are also the ones who observe end user reactions firsthand and get a better feel for what works and what does not. They are the first to note user behavior in information gathering, and they need to share this information with the catalogers. In fact, instruction librarians can provide valuable information to catalogers about what users really want and how the catalog can be improved.

BREAKING BOUNDARIES

There are departments with which cataloging has rare contact. This does not need to be the case, as good metadata creation is important to the whole organization. Expanding directions in digital libraries also provide new opportunities for catalogers to exercise their reach. The boundaries between digitization and metadata creation are getting blurred.

Administration

The library administration has a big stake in a quality, attractive, elegant online catalog. It is incumbent on cataloging managers to educate administrators in the capabilities of the catalog, its data generation potential, and its use as a public relations tool. For example, local records can be customized to display donor information, or they can be branded to highlight the library or any of its services. As a statistical data source, the catalog is an invaluable tool as well. And, last but not least, since online catalogs are usually freely accessible on the Internet, a good catalog is great advertising for the library.

Digital Libraries

Metadata and digitization go hand in hand. There are many opportunities for catalogers to collaborate in digital initiatives. From the moment a digital object is created, whether "born digital" or scanned, capture of metadata is important and catalogers can play an important role.

Often, such projects spring up in the libraries in departments other than cataloging, and catalogers are not involved, at least not early in the planning process. It is critical for the catalog manager to change this. Even if catalogers must learn new metadata schema to participate, they bring critical knowledge of information organization and analytical skills to digitization efforts.

Outreach is an important avenue to involvement in digitization and digital archiving. The catalog manager needs to learn who in the organization initiates digital projects and who may want to initiate them. Unlike other library functions, digital projects may not be relegated to a single department.

Flexibility is yet again an important skill. Remember that MARC may not be the best markup scheme to serve a digital project, at least not up front (MARC may be valuable later on to publicize a digital collection in WorldCat and other discovery tools). Your communications and collaboration will break down if the interaction ends up reinforcing the rigid cataloger stereotype that insists on doing things the way "we've always done them." Involvement in digital projects leads to job enrichment, giving catalogers opportunities to learn new standards and applications.

BUILDING THE SKILL SET

It is easy to say that collaboration is good for the library organization, and that catalogers should take active part. Actually making it happen is a different story, and a challenge for the manager.

Communication skills have been frequently mentioned in this chapter. As a key to collaboration, the listening half of communication is as important as expressing yourself to colleagues clearly. We have noted that each library specialty has its own jargon—so make certain that you have not just heard your colleagues but understood them as well.

Collaboration is a two-way street. Each party needs to make its needs and expectations clear while at the same time being aware of the other party's needs and expectations. This mutual understanding and awareness makes it much easier to set realistic goals and to achieve them. This will also reduce misunderstandings, as each unit will be aware of what is possible, what is not, and why certain practices or results are not feasible.

Ultimately, collaboration is not a choice but a necessity. For any operation to stay relevant to the organization and to continue to provide value to the organization, it needs to integrate itself fully within the functions of all the other units and to have its functions fully articulated and coordinated with them.

This integration also provides the necessary feedback for adapting its work to serve the organization. A unit that works in isolation can quickly become irrelevant and useless, while a unit that collaborates becomes vital.

Managers must hone their communication skills every day, but it is still possible that working catalogers can experience much of their workday by talking to no one else but other catalogers. The manager should make it a priority to give catalogers opportunities to improve their communication skills so that they can meet with better success when working with colleagues outside the department. If members of your department need some practice at this, give them strategic opportunities to practice theses skills. Perhaps start out with a collaborative project within the department before branching outside.

By collaborating more actively and effectively, catalogers will be able to better support the mission of the library. They might break a few stereotypes in the process, too.

REFERENCES

Gregory, J. M., A. I. Weber, and S. R. Dippie. "Innovative Roles for Technical Services Librarians: Extending Our Reach." *Technical Services Quarterly* 25 (2008): 4, 37–47.
Steele, T. "The New Cooperative Cataloging." *Library Hi Tech* 27 (2009): 1, 68–77.

CHAPTER 8

MARC: A New Life through Reusing and Remixing

Glen Wiley

Machine Readable Cataloging (MARC) has long been the library standard for sharing and organizing resource description. MARC provides well-structured, consistent, and coded records for bibliographic, holdings, and authority data used by humans and machines alike. Exploiting the richness of the MARC standard in venues beyond the integrated library system (ILS) is a strategy for using our existing resources to interact with new discovery tools. This chapter surveys the ways MARC has been reused outside the ILS by diverse libraries. It also examines an approach to project management for repurposing MARC to new formats.

SURVEY OF MARC REUSED OUTSIDE THE ILS

MARC is reused in many forms outside of the ILS for a variety of reasons. Some libraries have mapped MARC to a new database structure to accommodate for a change or upgrade in an existing system. One of the most common ways of doing this is to map MARC to an Extensible Markup Language (XML)-based metadata standard. XML is widely used in information systems and understood by many platforms. Others have created new collections of digital materials and ingested preexisting metadata into another system. Some libraries have shared their MARC metadata with a wider information community; some have improved interoperability by expressing it in XML. MARC is also being worked with the semantic Web and linked data community. With linked data, users are no longer limited to searching based on relationships that have been predefined by application developers, database designers, or librarians; users can create and search based on relationships that are meaningful to them. The possible reuses of MARC are potentially limitless.

We will never all use the same metadata formats. For this reason, we need to be able to remix and reuse our data from whatever form it originates. It does not matter how bibliographic metadata are stored as long as such data can be presented in any format requested.

LARGE-SCALE DIGITIZATION MATERIALS

Many large public and academic libraries have begun the digitization of millions of books under programs such as Google Book Search and Microsoft Live Search Books. The aim of these large-scale projects is bring copyright-free content accessible to the world. While the optical character recognition (OCR) text from the digital books can be one avenue of access to these materials, the existing MARC data for the titles and has provided an additional avenue of discovery to these materials for the end user.

For example, Cornell University Library has made print-on-demand books available for many of its digitized out-of-copyright books. These books are then made available for online ordering in conjunction with BookSurge, a subsidiary of Amazon. The printer is supplied with metadata from the MARC bibliographic record in order to produce book covers and other descriptive information about the digital content. In order to prepare its print-on-demand books, Cornell had to create a comprehensive list of bibliographic identifiers, titles, authors, and other fields derived from MARC data and transform that data into the ONline Information eXchange (ONIX) standard. ONIX is an XML-based standard used widely in the publishing industry.

While metadata specifications for large-scale digitization initiatives are not well documented or publicized because of nondisclosure agreements, there are some other examples of descriptive, structural, administrative, and preservation metadata that have reused MARC metadata that we can examine. In the case of the Google Book Search Project, the University of Michigan Library created descriptive metadata based on MARC records (Rieger 2008, 17). Cornell University Library used the Metadata Transmission and Encoding Standard (METS) for its digitization projects with Microsoft. The METS schema was used for recording MARC and mandatory fields of the PREservation Metadata: Implementation Strategies (PREMIS) scheme for preservation metadata. The Open Content Alliance uses bibliographic metadata in MARC binary as well as MARCXML and Dublin Core for descriptive metadata purposes (Rieger 2008, 17). Some participating libraries in Egypt, China, and India have used MARC descriptive metadata for the Million Book Project (Rieger 2008, 17).

Libraries have poured much effort over the years into MARC metadata. Many of these large-scale digitization projects rely on harvesting bibliographic information from MARC records in local catalogs. Doing so offers a long-term return on the investment made in MARC bibliographic data.

ELECTRONIC RESOURCES AND DIGITAL PORTALS

The display, description, access, and management of electronic resources is an evolving art. Many libraries still catalog the majority of resources (either electronic or physical) in MARC. Usually, catalog displays from MARC records are not the only or best answers for accessing these electronic resources for our users. Many libraries have sought out alternative displays based on MARC data to highlight and organize electronic resources. Colorado College's Tutt Library repurposed MARC records to build electronic database lists on its library's website (Ou and Gregory 2007, 52). The library created dynamic pages of electronic databases automatically populated with MARC data and reduced the number of places in these databases that library staff would need to manage updates. The process of using the MARC data required a new cataloging work flow to aid the scripts to create the Web pages. Once the records were cataloged in MARC, scripts (using MySQL language) automatically generated the Web pages (Ou and Gregory 2007, 54).

As another example, Cornell University Library used MARC subfields to support access to MARC-derived Dublin Core records in its ENCompass-based "Find Articles/Find Databases/Find e-Journals" system. Staff working on the ENCompass Project consulted with a generic MARC–to–Dublin Core crosswalk and adjusted the crosswalk regularly throughout the project to meet their needs. Then they documented the revised crosswalk. This enabled Cornell staff to offer their MARC mapping scheme to other libraries. These efforts were Cornell's first attempts to record a generalized MARC-based scheme and the application-specific mapping derived from it.

Other libraries are using MARC data in non-ILS portals to display growing numbers of electronic resources more prominently, allowing them to feature institutional repository items and digital library items alongside traditional library materials. These portals force libraries to process, index, and harvest MARC data into new discovery tools beyond the traditional catalog. The University of Virginia's Project Blacklight highlights this approach to a single-search interface for aggregated digital content that would otherwise require separate searches for each system (Sadler 2009, 57). In such cases, the MARC data become part of an XML-based metadata to support new discovery functions for the user.

THE SEMANTIC WEB AND LINKED DATA

"Linked data" is "a term used to describe a recommended best practice for exposing, sharing, and connecting pieces of data, information, and knowledge on the Semantic Web using URIs and RDF" (Wikipedia 2010). Linked data allow any user on the Web to create a customized view of data to satisfy different job roles and changing needs. The idea would be to build a community that helps, curates, and interconnects the data as needed. MARC data has so many trusted subjects, place-names, personal names, and terms that it is an excellent building block for linked data systems. One instance is an experiment at Stanford that employed 175,000 MARC records for music material and identified and graphed the relationships between unique access points (Persons 2008).

SPECIALIZED DIGITAL LIBRARY PROJECTS

As librarians create new digital collections, the integration of preexisting metadata like MARC can greatly increase the cost-effectiveness and efficiency of a project. There are creative ways to make use of machine-readable metadata for item- or collection-level MARC records both inside and outside of an institution's ILS. Less-than-full-level MARC records may not meet a given library's needs and standards for the traditional catalog but may be worth using in a different context, such as a new acquisitions list where title and creator are all that is needed.

Cornell University Library derived metadata from MARC records for many of its digital library projects. In 1995–1996, for one of Cornell's earliest and largest digital conversion projects, The Making of America, the library supplied its scanning vendor with MARC records. In turn, the vendor created volume-level descriptive metadata records to accompany digitized page images. Project staff relied on the MARC-derived metadata primarily for file management, but they also applied it in an early online delivery system. A number of Cornell projects completed since then have used metadata derived from MARC records and mapped into Text Encoding Initiative Lite documents. These projects include the Core Historical Literature of Agriculture, the Samuel J. May Anti-Slavery Collection, Historical Math Monographs, and the Home Economics Archive. Each project required a different mapping schema, but all these projects were similar in how they used MARC records.

PROJECT MANAGEMENT FOR REPURPOSING MARC

Libraries have a tremendous source of metadata in their in-house systems that are key to accessing their collections. As libraries continue to use third-party metadata from multiple sources, mapping and transformation work become increasingly a part of our regular workload. Careful management of metadata can hopefully avoid complex maintenance work in the future or having differing metadata records for the same resources (Kurth 2004, 154).

Adopting a coordinated, project management-based approach will lead to better library metadata management. MARC metadata repurposing touches many areas of the library: cataloging, public services, and information technology staff in libraries of all sizes and configurations should be engaged in these activities for best results. Specific library configurations and activities will drive the exact work flow of a MARC repurposing project. However, there are some generalizations and approaches to all MARC repurposing projects that will improve library metadata and technical services management.

When using MARC outside the ILS, mindful metadata processing requires five components:

- The consulting process of advising and deciding on the metadata schema, vocabularies, and content standards
- A design phase in which one must determine which metadata fields will be used, displayed, and possibly indexed in a new system
- Definition of the relationships between metadata schemes, or mapping, and the determination of how the data should be presented in its new context
- The production stage, where the metadata are moved between two schema
- The creation of access control and metadata management

The following sections offer practical next steps for practitioners who wish to apply project management to their metadata operations.

CONSULTING

Consultation it is an important part of the process in any metadata project, especially MARC repurposing. Communication and planning are always a critical part to project management that can get overlooked at the start when one is anxious to begin work.

It is important from the beginning to set a broad goal among stakeholders. The stakeholders could include catalogers, public services staff, programmers, users, technical services managers, curators of a digital collection, faculty members, and other community partners. In the consulting stage, many critical details should be established between all parties involved. These details should be time lines, goals, metadata schemas, selection of vocabularies, content standards, sources of metadata, expertise available and required, and technology needs. All stakeholders in the project should be a part of the consulting process. An agreement on the project details and shared goals between all stakeholders will make the rest of the stages of the project easier to accomplish in the time frame established.

DESIGN

The design process involves determining which metadata fields to use, how to display the metadata in the output, and which metadata will be indexed in a new system. Depending on the desired end result, each repurposing of the MARC metadata will entail different design decisions, depending on whether it will be intended to be used in the semantic environment, a digital library system, or a Web page display. The new remix of MARC data will need to be consistent and predictable for the new software system, transmission files, and the end user.

Two stakeholders in particular are critical to this design stage of the project. The first is the cataloger who understands MARC data. Most often, a MARC cataloger will understand the content standards and standard vocabularies by which the metadata were created. This cataloger will then understand how to reuse those metadata in an optimal, intelligent way. For example, strings of names from MARC fields might be ordered oddly in separate fields in the MARC record or ambiguously separated with punctuation. The cataloger will decide if those orders of names are appropriate to use in the new output or if the MARC metadata are unpredictable and/or insufficient to the new output's needs. During this design process, the cataloger may investigate other sources of metadata for the names rather than the MARC records in the catalog.

The second stakeholder important to the design process is the person responsible for managing the next use of the metadata. Whether that person is the programmer who understands the ingestion of metadata needed or the end user who wants to see his or her resources in a repository, this role is critical to success in the design stage and the project's success.

MAPPING

While the design process can overlap with activities found in the mapping stage, the design process is based primarily on planning rather than action. By contrast, the actual movement of each MARC element or field into its new metadata schemas is called "mapping" or "crosswalking." The goals are to establish relationships between semantically equivalent elements in different metadata schemes and to produce a plan to map or crosswalk these metadata relationships (St Pierre and LaPlant 1998; Woodley 2000).

Since there are a number of MARC-to-other schema maps available, it is often best to try to work with these first as a helpful starting point. Such mappings are available out on the Web. When working with an existing mapping, a library might see the need to go beyond the existing outline to meet the goals of the project. One reason to extend the mapping is if the Library of Congress map did not address all MARC fields and subfields and the library wanted to use a greater number of these. Another reason might be that the library wanted to expand the "Notes" section of the Library of Congress mapping to reflect its own library's practices with regard to such decisions as the treatment of initial articles in titles.

There are many issues that one may encounter when mapping MARC metadata to another other metadata schema. For example, collapsing different types of information in one field, as is common in MARC–to–Dublin Core mapping, causes a loss of specificity. In your new metadata schema, you may want a statement that combines information from the MARC description field, notes field, and/or copyright date field. Or you may need to parse these pieces of information in separate Dublin Core fields. A different challenge arises when not all the MARC records in your data set have the same amount of information or lack certain information, such as a series statement. There can also be clear differences in semantics. For example, date fields can be problematic to map, as the publication date in the 260 field of a MARC record may not translate well to another schema that is based on the date of the creation of the work.

The absence of corresponding elements in another schema can be problematic. You might think it is important to retain the MARC 250 field that states the edition statement, but it does not have a direct parallel field in the new schema, as in simple Dublin Core. In addition, MARC records may not have information that is pertinent to the digital version of a resource. An example of this would be rights information or source information. Accounting for changes of local MARC coding practice over time can also be troublesome to deal with when working with records created over many years. And simple human error is unavoidable in any batch of MARC records: missing of subfield codes, double entry, use of the 856 field instead of the 962 field, and inconsistent 246 field indicators are examples of human errors.

Once the mapping issues have been addressed, it is important to document the decisions made in the process. Documentation will provide a finalized view of all mapping decisions. Access to the project's standard mapping scheme shared between all stakeholders is important. These maps can be stored on a shared library drive, a staff website, a wiki, or any other means of shared access. These specific mapping schemes developed for particular projects will create a wealth of metadata history decisions within your library. The documentation will be critical in the future for other MARC repurposing or metadata decisions, including software migrations.

PRODUCTION

Once the metadata map has been created, production can begin. At this stage, item- or collection-level metadata are created through a transformation process. Metadata transformation is the design and implementation of scripts and other tools that move mapped metadata between schemes (Kurth 2004, 157).

The first option for an automated process of MARC to a new metadata schema is to employ a custom transformation script in the MARC data set. Scripting is a common approach to transformations. Implementing this transformation process might involve an information technology staff, depending on each cataloger's skill level with common programming languages like Perl, Java, or others. The library will use the mapping to identify and extract fields from the MARC records. The extracted data will then usually be encoded in XML-based format and stored. Once the script is written and used in the transformation process, the operation can then move quickly.

This production process of using a transformation script is a good choice for many situations. If the mapping needs refinement, the production process with a script can be easily updated to include mapping changes and run again on the MARC data set. Any MARC field can be extracted into the MARC record file and mapped to almost any metadata output format based on the scripted specification. These scripts can be reused over time, as they can are easily adapted to new but similar projects.

However, while this scripted approach to metadata transformations does allow for many modifications over time, these modifications may require a programmer. As a result, these modifications can be costly to the process, strain library resources, and cause delayed time lines for the project. In addition, each script is a project specific, so multiple projects could require extensive modifications to achieve the desired mapping and results. The scale of the project can be a deciding factor when choosing your production work and transformation process.

A second production option is to use an EXtensible Stylesheet Language (XSLT). Style sheet processing essentially converts one XML document into another XML document by using instructions contained in the style sheet. Using a style sheet, many variations can be made easily and conveniently. The basic ability to make XSLT style sheet alterations consists of skills that cataloging staff can learn through training courses and practice. If the cataloger has prepared the mapping for the metadata, the style sheet work and alterations can become straightforward to accommodate the project's needs. For libraries, entire MARC records would be extracted from their system and converted to the MARCXML standard. A style sheet can manipulate and transform the MARCXML metadata to create an HTML page out of the MARC data or display the transformation from MARCXML to another metadata format (Keith 2004, 124).

In some instances, programming support may be needed to initially create an XSLT transformation tool, but then library staff can make changes with a little assistance from application developers (Keith 2004, 125). Developed in the 1990s, MARCXML can be useful for repurposing MARC to play with network protocols like Open Archives Initiative (Elings and Waibel 2007, 5). The Library of Congress hosts a MARC-to-MARCXML tool. Additionally, MarcEdit is an open-source tool that can transform raw MARC files to multiple standards using style sheets (Reese 2004, 26). Employing one of these tools can be cost effective and flexible. These XSLT transformations can handle small sets of records, single-record transformations, and large-scale projects. Like scripts, XSLT transformation tools can be reused for other MARC projects.

MARC metadata transformation work will inevitably require variations in every project. Transformation processes must accommodate these as a functional requirement in their design. To transform MARC metadata in a technically and economically efficient manner, the processes must be broadly available to cataloging and library staff rather than delegated solely to information technology units. Libraries engaged in MARC repurposing need decentralized transformation processes that cataloging staff can easily modify through routine and standardized methods, such as the alteration or addition of XSLT style sheets.

There are other approaches beyond library-specific scripts and XSLT transformations. There are ready-made software tools to aid in the process of reuse and harvesting MARC metadata. Some of these MARC tools available are MARCEdit, MARC Report, and OCLC's Connexion Metadata Extraction tool. These tools can create scripting solutions for transforming metadata, convert data into MARC from common delimited text files, and handle other special problems when converting records in or out of all versions of MARC. For more information on MARC specialized tools, the Library of Congress maintains a list of software programs on its website to use for various MARC records and systems (http://www.loc.gov/standards).

ACCESS AND MANAGEMENT

Providing access to resources is an overarching goal in each stage of the MARC repurposing process. However, it is important to evaluate the access level of the resources described after the production and transformation process is done. Quality control for irregularities in the data should be performed at this stage. Metadata user communities like METS and Dublin Core share their experiences and tools with their websites and electronic mailing lists. It is important that each library that transforms and reuses MARC metadata or other metadata create a public space to share these experiences and work. Too often, libraries devise metadata maps, write transformation scripts, and create intermediate metadata files to meet project goals and deadlines without consulting with others.

A documentation library of MARC repurposing processes would have an inventory of the data files, mapping schematics, transformation processes, and systems that make up the components of the library's current metadata repurposing efforts. A sample documentation library of MARC metadata repurposing activities could include the following:

- The original MARC bibliographic metadata
- Extract scripts or tools used to select the MARC for the project
- The XML metadata collection and storage scheme
- The transformation scripts
- XML output files
- Validation tools

Reusing MARC and other metadata operations would grow more effectively if libraries were to develop metadata processes that promoted sharing and reuse.

CONCLUSION

MARC metadata are a valuable resource for making information more easily discovered. With each project to reuse MARC metadata, there are considerations and practices to follow for success. First, do the consulting and investigation work. This work will include setting goals, giving time lines, setting forth resources, and establishing costs and benefits of undertaking a MARC mapping and transformation process. This first step will need consensus from all stakeholders. Next, design your metadata and mapping for the specific-use case of the project. Production and transformation processes will follow using custom or freely available tools to create the metadata for a new use. Finally, double-check your goals and the quality of the end results. All your MARC repurposing project work can be shared within your library as well as with the wider library community through good communication and documentation.

By exposing our MARC metadata in new ways and structures, we open the new avenues for the information about library resources. New audiences beyond the library community can provoke new thoughts about old information. MARC in new metadata schemas can be molded and manipulated not only by programmers, application developers, and other information technology workers but also by catalogers and metadata staff. The ideas presented in this chapter are beginning steps and tools to effective project management with MARC metadata reuse and remix.

REFERENCES

Elings, Mary W., and Gunter Waibel. "Metadata for All: Descriptive Standards and Metadata Sharing across Libraries, Archives and Museums." *First Monday* 12, no. 3 (2007): 1–12.

Keith, Corey. "Using XSLT to Manipulate MARC Metadata." *Library Hi Tech* 22, no. 2 (2004): 122–30.

Kurth, Martin, David Ruddy, and Nathan Rupp. "Repurposing MARC Metadata: Using Digital Project Experience to Develop a Metadata Management Design." *Library Hi Tech* 22, no. 2 (2004): 153–65.

Ou, Carol, and Gwen Gregory. "Old Wine in New Bottles: Repurposing MARC Records for Electronic Databases." *Against the Grain* 19, no. 5 (2007): 52–56.

Persons, Jerry. "Titles and Places and Names! Oh My!—and Experimental Graph of a Library Catalog." Paper presented at the Digital Library Federation Fall Forum, Providence, Rhode Island, November 13, 2008.

Reese, Terry. "MarcEdit Suite." *Computers in Libraries* 7 (2004): 24–28.

Rieger, Oya. "Preservation in the Age of Large-Scale Digitization: A White Paper." Council on Library and Information Resources. 2008. http://www.clir.org/pubs/reports/pub141/pub141.pdf (accessed December 8, 2009).

Sadler, Elizabeth. "Project Blacklight: A Next Generation Library Catalog at a First Generation University." *Library Hi Tech* 27, no. 1 (2009): 57–67.

St Pierre, Margaret, and William P. LaPlant Jr. "Issues in Crosswalking Content Metadata Standards." 1998. http://www.niso.org/publications/white_papers/crosswalk (accessed June 1, 2010).

Wikipedia. "Linked Data." *Wikipedia, the Free Encyclopedia*. 2010. http://en.wikipedia.org/wiki/Linked_Data (accessed March 23, 2010).

Woodley, Mary S. *Crosswalks: The Path to Universal Access?* Edited by Martha Baca. Los Angeles: Getty Research Institute, 2000.

CHAPTER 9

Moving Ahead with Metadata: Adding Value through Grant-Funded Projects

Amy S. Jackson

External funding agencies have always been an important source of support for library projects. The Institute of Museum and Library Services, the National Endowment for the Humanities, the National Science Foundation, and the Andrew W. Mellon Foundation are just a few of the many agencies that provide grants to libraries. However, grants, especially large grants, are very competitive, and reviewers need to know that the requesting institution is capable of spending the funding institution's money wisely. Grant proposals should demonstrate knowledge of similar projects in the library community, how the proposed project will fit into the larger cultural heritage community, and the intended national impact of the award.

In accordance with President Obama's Memorandum on Transparency and Open Government (White House 2009), federal agencies are beginning to require that research and resources funded by federal grant money be made freely available to the public. Libraries have always operated with the goal of making their resources findable to as many people as possible, and this new interest in government transparency fits well with general library practice. However, just because a document is made publicly available does not mean that the public will be able to find this document. In order to achieve a high level of findability, our resources must have high-quality metadata describing them. Good metadata will encourage use of our resources and demonstrate that we are using grant money to better the general population.

Although special collections departments generally provide materials for digital library grant projects, these projects are an excellent opportunity for the cataloging department to collaborate with the special collections department and other units involved in a project and demonstrate added value to the library. The materials selected for digitization need high-quality descriptive records, and cataloging departments are already well positioned to take on this role. As traditional cataloging work flows are reevaluated and copy cataloging is more commonly purchased from vendors, these projects are an excellent place to turn for good use of cataloging skills and to demonstrate value to the library. However, in order to create these descriptive records, the cataloging department must be up to date with metadata standards.

METADATA FUNDAMENTALS

There are many types of metadata, often classified according to the purpose for which it will serve. In *Metadata Fundamentals for All Librarians*, Patricia Caplan (2003) identifies three main types of metadata: descriptive, administrative, and structural. Descriptive metadata help a user with the four Functional Requirements for Bibliographic Records tasks of find, identify, select, and obtain (IFLA Study Group on the Functional Requirements for Bibliographic Records 1998). Administrative metadata helps manage the life cycle of a resource and can include information such as how a resource was created, subsequent processing of the resource, and rights to the resource. Subclasses of administrative metadata include technical metadata and rights metadata. Technical metadata can include information such as scanning equipment and processing information, and rights metadata explicitly state under what circumstances the resource may be used. The final main type of metadata, structural metadata, defines how resources are related and is generally intended to be machine readable. For example, a digital library navigation system displaying a digital book made up of multiple image files—an image for each page—needs to understand the order in which the files should be displayed. The system reads the structural metadata and displays the images in the proper order.

Additionally, some metadata are intended to be embedded into the file directly, while other metadata are stored separately. Technical metadata are most often embedded in the file. For example, digital cameras embed technical information about time, date, camera model, and, depending on the camera, focal range and sometimes even GPS coordinates directly into the image file. Descriptive metadata are normally stored independently from the resource and linked to the file through an identifier, just as a Machine Readable Cataloging (MARC) record for a physical book is stored in the catalog and linked to the book through identification information (Online Computer Library Center numbers, ISBN numbers, and so on).

This chapter addresses the types of metadata that a cataloging department is most likely to encounter: descriptive metadata stored separately from the resource and, in the case of digital resources, usually linked to the resource by an identifier. An in-depth discussion of each standard is not within the scope of this chapter, but citations to each standard are provided for more information.

DESCRIPTIVE METADATA

Descriptive practices across the cultural heritage community (libraries, archives, and museums) have developed differently because of the different types of materials and institutional missions. However, it is important to understand what these practices have in common and when a practice from a different community may be more appropriate for your material.

Descriptive metadata standards can be broken down into the roles that they play in describing the content. Common descriptive metadata standards include data structure, data content, data value, data format, and data exchange standards. In *Descriptive Metadata Guidelines for RLG Cultural Materials* (RLG 2005), a metaphor is used comparing metadata records to a case of bottles being filled, stored, and delivered (see also Elings and Waibel 2007).

According to the metaphor, the structure of a metadata record is similar to an empty bottle. The bottle provides structure but is meaningless by itself. Metadata structure in the bibliographic community is specified by the MARC format. MARC defines the fields but does not indicate how the fields should be used. Other metadata formats defining the structure of a record include the Dublin Core Metadata Element Set (Dublin Core Metadata Initiative 2008), Categories for the Description of Works of Art (CDWA) (J. Paul Getty Trust and College Art Association 2006), Visual Resources Association (VRA) Core 4.0 (Visual Resources Association 2007), and Encoded Archival Description (EAD) (Library of Congress 2002). Metadata structure formats (or schemas) are often mapped to other formats when records are being shared across platforms. Dublin Core is often referred to as the "lowest common denominator" among these schemas because it has fewer fields than other schemas and less stringent content guidelines. Most metadata schemas have standard crosswalks to Dublin Core, and Dublin Core is a required format for exporting records through the Open Archives Initiative Protocol for Metadata Harvesting (OAI-PMH). However, Dublin Core is not as rich as the other schemas and may not be appropriate to describe digital library objects initially.

Continuing with the bottle metaphor, the content of a metadata record is like the liquid inside a bottle. The liquid has no form without the bottle, just as the content of a metadata record has no meaning without a data structure. Data content in the bibliographic community is defined by the Anglo-American Cataloguing Rules, Second Edition (AACR2; or RDA in the future). Other data content standards include *Cataloging Cultural Objects* (CCO) (Baca et al. 2006) and *Describing Archives: A Content Standard* (DACS; Society of American Archivists 2004).

Data value standards are the controlled vocabularies that most librarians are familiar with. The bibliographic community relies on the *Library of Congress Subject Headings* (LCSH) and the *Name Authority File* (NAF). There are many other lists of controlled vocabularies used in the cultural heritage community, including the "Art & Architecture Thesaurus" (AAT; J. Paul Getty Trust 2010a), the "Union List of Artist Names" (J. Paul Getty Trust 2010c), the "Thesaurus of Geographic Names" (TGN; J. Paul Getty Trust 2010b), and the "Thesaurus for Graphic Materials" (TGM; Library of Congress 1995).

Additionally, some projects create their own controlled vocabulary lists; however, this should be undertaken with care because local controlled vocabulary lists may not be interoperable with other projects.

The data format supported by most metadata schemas is XML (Extensible Markup Language). In the bottle analogy, the data format is a box holding many different bottles. XML binds together elements from a structure standard and allows elements to be arranged hierarchically. Most library cataloging tools automatically create the XML markup from a record a cataloger has created. The cultural heritage community has many different XML instantiations that support our metadata structure standards, such as MARCXML, VRA Core 4.0, EAD, MODS, and CDWA Lite XML.

Data exchange standards allow XML records to be exchanged between institutions. The standards currently used in the cultural heritage community are OAI-PMH, Z39.50, and SRU/SRW. OAI-PMH is a protocol allowing institutions to collect (or harvest) XML records created by other institutions and combine them into a single database for searching and/or browsing. OAI-PMH requires that metadata be supplied in Dublin Core and also allows the same metadata records to be provided in richer formats. For a detailed discussion of OAI-PMH, see *Using the Open Archives Initiatives Protocol for Metadata Harvesting* (Cole and Foulonneau 2007). Z39.50 and SRU/ SRW are protocols that allow searching across multiple remote databases simultaneously and are commonly referred to as metasearch. These protocols are most often used with commercial databases to which a library subscribes. The type of materials and databases being searched across determines the most appropriate data exchange standard.

How do all these metadata standards relate? Following are some basic examples of descriptive metadata standards being used together to provide greater access to cultural heritage materials:

- A library book is described using MARC for structure, AACR2 for content, LCSH and the NAF for value (subject and author fields), XML for format (MARCXML), and OAI-PMH for exchange.
- A sculpture is described using CDWA for structure, CCO for content, AAT and TGN for value (subject and location fields), XML for format (CDWA Lite XML), and OAI-PMH for exchange.
- An archival finding aid is described using EAD for structure, DACS for content, LCSH for value (subject fields), XML for format (EAD), and OAI-PMH for exchange.
- A photograph is described using Dublin Core for structure, AACR2 for content, LCSH for value (subject fields), XML for format (oai_dc), and OAI-PMH for exchange.

Every project should strive to create high-quality metadata using the types of standards described here. Library grant applicants should have these standards in mind when planning projects, as grant-funding agencies will want to know that their money is being used to support projects that employ national standards.

WHAT ELSE DO I NEED TO KNOW ABOUT METADATA TO HELP MY GRANT APPLICATION?

Without high-quality metadata, library resources are hard to find, and a digital file stored in a server may never be found again. Funding agencies want to know that their money will be used appropriately and that many people will benefit from their funded projects. According to the 2010 National Leadership Grants *Grant Program Guidelines* of the Institute of Museum and Library Services (2009), one of the criteria that reviewers look for is "evidence that the project demonstrates interoperability and accessibility in its broadest context and potential for integration into larger scale initiatives" (30). Metadata that are created according to national standards are highly accessible to service providers, allowing integration with and access to your resources through portals having national scope such as WorldCat (previously OAIster) and subject portals such as the National Science Digital Library (http://nsdl.org) and Opening History (http://imlsdcc.grainger.uiuc.edu/history).

Several U.S. government organizations have created digital library guidelines that often include metadata guidelines. Grant applicants should be aware of these guidelines as they plan their digital collections. The National Information Standards Organization (NISO 2007) published *A Framework of Guidance for Building Good Digital Collections* with the following metadata recommendations for well-planned digital collections:

- Metadata Principle 1: Good metadata conform to community standards in a way that is appropriate to the materials in the collection, users of the collection, and current and potential future uses of the collection.

- Metadata Principle 2: Good metadata support interoperability.

- Metadata Principle 3: Good metadata use authority control and content standards to describe objects and collocate related objects.

- Metadata Principle 4: Good metadata include a clear statement of the conditions and terms of use for the digital object.

- Metadata Principle 5: Good metadata support the long-term curation and preservation of objects in collections.

- Metadata Principle 6: Good metadata records are objects themselves and therefore should have the qualities of good objects, including authority, authenticity, archivability, persistence, and unique identification.

Other guidelines include *Understanding Metadata* (NISO 2004), the "Federal Agencies Digitization Guidelines Initiative" (2010), and *Metadata Demystified: A Guide for Publishers* (Brand, Daly, and Meyers 2003).

Metadata can also be used as a marketing and dissemination tool. By planning to expose your digital collection's metadata to harvesters, you are demonstrating that the institution is willing share its resources with a larger pool of users than its normal user base. Harvesters will combine the metadata with metadata from other collections to allow users to search across multiple collections simultaneously. When users find a metadata record pointing to a resource that they are interested in, the harvester will send them directly to the original resource at the home collection, thus driving traffic to the collection's website. This situation is beneficial to the library, the users, and the grant-funding agency.

What standards are grant-funded projects following? In 2007, the Digital Collections and Content project, funded by the Institute of Museum and Library Services (IMLS), reported an increase in the number of IMLS-funded digital collections using Dublin Core (Palmer, Zavalina, and Mustafoff 2007). This increase may be due to the growing popularity of software with built-in support for OAI-PMH and thus requiring use of Dublin Core or the perceived ease of use of Dublin Core. Locally developed schemes were also popular, as were records created using the MARC standard. Dublin Core is always a good option as a lowest common denominator between schemas, but if richer metadata are available, data providers should attempt to make these metadata available for harvesting as well.

HOW TO CREATE METADATA FOR YOUR PROJECT

The first step for determining appropriate metadata for your grant-funded library project is to evaluate the types of material with which you will be working. As mentioned previously, different standards have developed for different material types, and sometimes several standards can be used simultaneously for the same material. In addition, one needs to take into account the level of granularity appropriate for the material. For example, if you are working with a collection of photographs, should every photograph be described individually, or would a collection description suffice? For a collection of historical photographs described at the item level, Dublin Core is generally appropriate, as is a local scheme that maps well to Dublin Core. If the photographs are of art images, VRA Core 4.0 may be more appropriate because the metadata fields are richer and more refined for detailed subject, location, and creator information. If the collection of photographs is large and the images are very similar, a collection description using EAD or the Dublin Core Collection Description Application Profile may provide enough information.

On a very practical level, the capabilities of your systems must also be taken into account when choosing an appropriate metadata schema. For example, CONTENTdm supports Dublin Core, the VRA Core elements (but not the XML schema), and locally developed elements. If the library's Online Public

Access Catalog will be used to store the metadata records, MARC may be a more appropriate choice.

Another point to consider when planning metadata for projects is the users of the resources. Users with a high degree of subject knowledge have different metadata requirements than users with general knowledge. For example, a collection of art images used by art historians needs to be described at an appropriate level for their subject expertise (e.g., knowledge of styles, materials, creators, and so on), whereas the same collection used by K–12 students should include general terms more familiar to young people. Different controlled vocabularies are appropriate for each use case scenario, and even different schemas can be appropriate (VRA Core 4.0 for art historians and Dublin Core for K–12 students). Collections intended to be used by several different groups should include descriptions that will be helpful to all user types.

Another practical concern is the subject expertise available in the cataloging department. A collection of art images needs an expert in art history in order to be fully cataloged in VRA Core 4.0. However, the more general fields of Dublin Core allow for a more general description, appropriate for a department with limited expertise.

Project planners should also consider which items should have metadata records. According to the one-to-one principle, "in general Dublin Core metadata describes one manifestation or version of a resource, rather than assuming that manifestations stand in for one another" (Hillman 2005, 1.2). Thus, different records should be created for both the digital item and the original physical item if the item is not born digital. Traditional MARC cataloging also deals with this issue when deciding if a digital item should have a different MARC record or if information about the digital item should be contained in the original record. VRA Core 4.0 is the only metadata schema designed to describe both originals and surrogates (work and image records). In reality, many Dublin Core records attempt to describe both the physical resource and the digital surrogate in the same record. This leads to misleading statements such as "Format: JPEG; 8 × 11 inches" (Shreeves et al. 2005) where a digital file is described as having a physical dimension.

After these points have been considered, it is time to choose the most appropriate metadata schema for your project. Grant-funding agencies will want to know that the project is following national standards, so it is highly recommended that you follow a standard metadata schema. If the project opts to use a locally developed schema, be sure that it maps well to a standard schema such as Dublin Core.

Creating metadata records is the next step, and project directors should ensure that metadata creators are familiar with the characteristics of shareable metadata. Shareable metadata is important because they allow metadata from different projects to be shared and searched across simultaneously. According to Shreeves, Riley, and Milewicz (2006), the characteristics of shareable metadata include the following six Cs:

- *Content* is optimized for sharing.
- Metadata within shared collections reflect *consistent* practices.
- Metadata are *coherent*.
- *Context* is provided.
- The metadata provider *communicates* with aggregators through direct or indirect means.
- Metadata and sharing mechanisms *conform* to standards.

Additionally, metadata creators should receive metadata training to ensure that they fully understand the complexities involved. Studies have shown that misunderstanding and misuse of metadata fields decreases the quality of metadata records (Jackson et al. 2008). There are several resources available for learning about shareable metadata, including *Best Practices for OAI PMH Data Provider Implementations and Shareable Metadata* (Shreeves, Riley, and Hagedorn 2007) and "Metadata for You and Me" (2008).

If a schema other than Dublin Core is used to describe your resources, metadata should be mapped to Dublin Core in order to facilitate sharing through OAI-PMH. Mapping errors are common when preparing metadata for OAI-PMH, and metadata librarians should ensure that local fields do not lose meaning when mapped to common standards such as Dublin Core (Han et al. 2009). Metadata librarians should also examine the actual content of metadata fields instead of relying on the semantic meanings of the fields during the mapping process (Jackson et al. 2008). Additional practical advice for mapping to Dublin Core is available in Beisler and Willis (2009).

Finally, ensure that your metadata are available to be harvested through OAI-PMH or other means. Common systems, such as CONTENTdm and DSpace, have built-in support to expose metadata through OAI-PMH, and several open-source solutions are also available online. Cole and Foulonneau's (2007) *Using the Open Archives Initiatives Protocol for Metadata Harvesting* provides detailed information about OAI-PMH, including technical and historical information. At the very least, project managers should make sure that their repository validates at the Open Archives Initiative Repository Explorer (http://re.cs.uct.ac.za) or similar service. Metadata librarians should also perform random quality checks on exported records to catch any obvious errors.

CONCLUSION

Descriptive metadata are an essential component of digital library projects, allowing resources to be easily discovered. Funding agencies need to know that high-quality metadata will be created with the money they provide to support digital library projects, ensuring that the resources in which they have invested will not fall into obscurity. The best way to create quality metadata is to follow national standards or at least be aware of how local practices relate to national standards. Grant reviewers will look for knowledge of national standards and basic understanding of metadata in the grant application, so be sure that this knowledge is demonstrated in the narrative. Additionally, strong grant applications will address work flow and how metadata will be created over the course of the project. Finally, applicants should provide information about how collections and individual items will be optimized for discoverability, whether through metadata harvesting, registering in larger subject portals, or search engine optimization. An open approach to digital library projects following national standards will ensure grant-funding agencies quality projects in which they can invest their grant money.

Cataloging departments that are aware of and follow national metadata standards will be well positioned for other library departments and institutional units to turn to for metadata expertise and advice. Advice may be sought by those preparing grant applications or by already funded projects looking for metadata help. When other library departments consider the cataloging department an essential component of grant project work flows, grant money may be directly allocated to the cataloging department. Library departments that contribute to library funding and bring value to other departments will be encouraged to evolve and grow, even in difficult economic environments.

REFERENCES

Baca, Murtha, Patricia Harpring, Elisa Lanzi, Linda McRae, and Ann Baird Whiteside. *Cataloging Cultural Objects: A Guide to Describing Cultural Works and Their Images*. Chicago: ALA Editions, 2006.

Beisler, Amalia, and Glee Willis. "Beyond Theory: Preparing Dublin Core Metadata for OAI-PMH Harvesting." *Journal of Library Metadata* 9, no. 1 (2009): 65–97.

Brand, Amy, Frank Daly, and Barbara Meyers. *Metadata Demystified: A Guide for Publishers*. Bethesda, MD: Sheridan Press and NISO Press, 2003. Available at http://www.niso.org/standards/resources/Metadata_Demystified .pdf (retrieved January 7, 2010).

Caplan, Priscilla. *Metadata Fundamentals for All Librarians*. Chicago: American Library Association, 2003.

Cole, Timothy W., and Muriel Foulonneau. *Using the Open Archives Initiative Protocol for Metadata Harvesting*. Westport, CT: Libraries Unlimited, 2007.

Dublin Core Metadata Initiative. "Dublin Core Metadata Element Set, Version 1.1." 2008. Available at http://dublincore.org/documents/dces (retrieved January 7, 2010).

Elings, Mary W., and Günter Waibel. "Metadata for All: Descriptive Standards and Metadata Sharing across Libraries, Archives and Museums." *First*

Monday 12, no. 3 (March 2007). Available at http://firstmonday.org/article/view/1628/1543 (retrieved January 7, 2010).

"Federal Agencies Digitization Guidelines Initiative." 2010. Available at http://www.digitizationguidelines.gov (retrieved January 7, 2010).

Han, Myung-Ja, Christine Cho, Timothy W. Cole, and Amy S. Jackson. "Metadata for Special Collections in CONTENTdm: How to Improve Interoperability of Unique Fields through OAI-PMH." *Journal of Library Metadata* 9, no. 3 (2009): 213–38.

Hillman, Diane. "Using Dublin Core." 2005. Available at http://dublincore.org/documents/usageguide (retrieved January 7, 2010).

IFLA Study Group on the Functional Requirements for Bibliographic Records. "Functional Requirements for Bibliographic Records: Final Report." 1998. Available at http://archive.ifla.org/VII/s13/frbr/frbr.htm (retrieved December 17, 2009).

Institute of Museum and Library Services. *2010 National Leadership Grants: Grant Program Guidelines, CFDA No. 43.312.* Washington, DC: Institute of Museum and Library Services, 2009. Available at http://www.imls.gov/applicants/grants/pdf/NLG_2010.pdf (retrieved January 7, 2010).

J. Paul Getty Trust. "Art and Architecture Thesaurus Online." 2010a. Available at http://www.getty.edu/research/conducting_research/vocabularies/aat (retrieved January 7, 2010).

J. Paul Getty Trust. "Thesaurus of Geographic Names Online." 2010b. Available at http://www.getty.edu/research/conducting_research/vocabularies/tgn (retrieved January 7, 2010).

J. Paul Getty Trust. "Union List of Artist Names Online." 2010c. Available at http://www.getty.edu/research/conducting_research/vocabularies/ulan (retrieved January 7, 2010).

J. Paul Getty Trust and College Art Association. "Categories for the Description of Works of Art." 2006. Available at http://www.getty.edu/research/conducting_research/standards/cdwa/index.html (retrieved January 7, 2010).

Jackson, Amy S., Myung-Ja Han, Kurt Groetsch, Megan Mustafoff, and Timothy W. Cole. "Dublin Core Metadata Harvested through OAI-PMH." *Journal of Library Metadata* 8, no. 1 (2008): 5–18.

Library of Congress. "EAD: Encoded Archival Description: Version 2002 Official Site." 2002. Available at http://www.loc.gov/ead (retrieved January 7, 2010).

Library of Congress. "Thesaurus for Graphic Materials I: Subject Terms." 2005. Available at http://www.loc.gov/rr/print/tgm1 (retrieved January 7, 2010).

"Metadata for you and me" (2008), available at http://images.library.uiuc.edu/projects/mym/index.html (retrieved January 7, 2010).

National Information Standards Organization. "A Framework of Guidance for Building Good Digital Collections." 3rd ed. 2007. Available at http://framework.niso.org/node/5 (retrieved December 18, 2009).

National Information Standards Organization. *Understanding Metadata.* Bethesda, MD: NISO Press, 2004. Available at http://www.niso.org/publications/press/UnderstandingMetadata.pdf (retrieved January 7, 2010).

Palmer, Carole L., Oksana Zavalina, and Megan Mustafoff. "Trends in Metadata Practices: A Longitudinal Study of Collection Federation." In *Proceedings of the 2007 Conference on Digital Libraries. International Conference on Digital Libraries, Vancouver, BC, Canada,* 386–95. New York: ACM Press, 2007.

RLG. *Descriptive Metadata Guidelines for RLG Cultural Materials.* 2005. Available at http://www.rlg.org/en/pdfs/RLG_desc_metadata.pdf (retrieved January 13, 2010).

Shreeves, Sarah L., Ellen M. Knutson, Besiki Stvilia, Carole L. Palmer, Michael B. Twidale, and Timothy W. Cole. "Is 'Quality' Metadata 'Shareable' Metadata? The Implication of Local Metadata Practice on Federated Collections." In *Proceedings of the Twelfth National Conference of the Association of College and Research Libraries, April 7–10 2005, Minneapolis, MN,* ed. H. A. Thompson, 223–37. Chicago: Association of College and Research Libraries, 2005.

Shreeves, Sarah L., Jenn Riley, and Kat Hagedorn, eds. *Best Practices for OAI PMH Data Provider Implementations and Shareable Metadata: DLF/NSDL Working Group on OAI PMH Best Practices.* Washington, DC: Digital Library Federation, 2007.

Shreeves, Sarah L., Jenn Riley, and Liz Milewicz. "Moving Towards Shareable Metadata." *First Monday* 11: 8 (August 2006). Available at http://firstmonday.org/issues/issue11_8/shreeves/index.html (retrieved January 7, 2010).

Society of American Archivists. *Describing Archives: A Content Standard.* Chicago: Society of American Archivists, 2004.

Visual Resources Association. "VRA Core 4.0." 2007. Available at http://www.vraweb.org/projects/vracore4 (retrieved January 7, 2010).

White House. "Transparency and Open Government." 2009. Available at http://www.whitehouse.gov/the_press_office/TransparencyandOpen Government (retrieved January 7, 2010).

Conclusion: Creating Collaborative Cataloging Communities in the Twenty-First Century

Rebecca L. Lubas

Cataloging departments have vital and varied roles to play in the twenty-first-century library, and they can do so by capitalizing and building on their traditions of practice. People notice, interpret, and retain information based on their values, assumptions, and expectations. Catalogers can take advantage of core shared values among themselves but must also look at how other communities view their services. Different values lead to the different ways of looking at the same thing (Agourran 2009, 130). Catalogers should look at how other library science specialties, patrons in the immediate service community, and patrons in a wider community seek information. After building a century of practice on consistency and uniformity, we must morph into a profession that has a set of guiding principles but with flexible manifestations. The Web 2.0 world is based on using and customizing information, and we need to incorporate consideration of these varied meanings in our work.

Information systems have built-in values that reflect where they were developed (Agourran 2009, 135). We may take the term "Anglo-American" out of the name of our core formal standard, but the original point of view will still remain and influence even though the vocabulary has expanded. One approach will be not to try live in denial of this heritage but rather to treat it as but one of many possible languages for organizing information. When the language one is using fails to meet the user needs, incorporate another standard (or language) or create new vocabulary within the language. In a community of practice, knowledge is continuously negotiated through processes of social interaction and networking (Kimble 2008, 461). This is how languages remain vital. It can be the same with the information profession's standards. An incarnation of this concept can be found in SwissBib. SwissBib is a "metacatalog" incorporating four languages, five

---

Ideas in this essay originally presented in a paper at the ISTEC *V International Symposium on Digital Libraries*, October 27, 2009 in Albuquerque, NM.

metadata standards, and 13 Online Public Access Catalogs (Viegener 2009, 18). The *Anglo-American Cataloguing Rules* play no small part in this huge database, but it is proof that we need not (indeed should not) remain monolingual, or monostandard.

In a successful community of practice, formal and informal interactions contribute to the success of the community (Sancho-Thomas 2009, 524). Directed learning can serve alongside peer interactions for the community's knowledge base development and technology transfer. Both competition and collaboration add to the vitality of the community and encourage richer social interactions that strengthen a community. Members of communities of practice have reported their communities benefiting in collaboration, idea creation, learning and development, professional identity, and trust between employees and colleagues (Fontaine and Millen 2004, 5). Certainly the cataloging profession can use these benefits.

In the past 15 years, metadata standards have multiplied and developed. These standards have not always come out of the library profession but rather have grown from specific information needs of specific communities. In addition to playing an active role in standards created by the library profession, catalogers should lend their expertise to other communities to help with the underlying architecture.

As we have examined, the changing role of the Library of Congress has impacted the cataloging departments dramatically. This de facto U.S. national library has undergone some serious institutional soul-searching and emerged by focusing its attention on its own collections. Like many of us, they are also coping with dramatic staff cuts. As we deal with this major shift in the center of our universe, we should take the opportunity to play a more active role in the shaping of our practices. A variation on the old chestnut, the lightbulb joke, goes "How many catalogers does it take to change a light bulb? Only one, but five have to call the Library of Congress to find out how to do it!" Let us change that perception and write the rules of changing the lightbulb for ourselves! While institutions like the Library of Congress will be key contributors to the community, we can be a richer, more robust community with fuller participation by more players.

In the single-standard world of the not-so-distant past, this often took the form of a very long apprenticeship phase of a new cataloger's career. Our profession could (and still does) look to experts with many decades of experience in the standards to do the teaching and interpretation for the apprentices and the journeymen. We now face the two major challenges to this model. First, many of those experts have retired or will retire in the next few years with a much smaller generation to replace them. Second, the multiplicity of quickly evolving standards makes the many years of training model impractical. With the need to learn multiple, quickly morphing standards, new skill sets are needed—flexibility and adaptability are now as important as precision and attention to detail. A more robust community of continuous learners needs to take the place of depth of skill in individuals with long cataloging careers.

We also need to find the right recipe for our databases. With e-books and other resources being purchased in packages of thousands, we can no longer afford to handcraft every piece of metadata. The twenty-first-century catalog manager needs to make decisions, such as when to choose packages of data from a vendor, when to outsource to a company or person with special expertise, and the very important decision of what materials are important and unique enough that your most precious resource—your local, human resources—should be allocated to create new metadata.

Catalogers have a somewhat undeserved reputation for being insular. We have been collaborating with our colleagues in acquisitions and collection development for many years, but now we can add a larger dimension to our collaboration. As libraries pick and choose where to develop collections and services, metadata creators can help drive the workings of those services and should be actively getting in on the ground floor of decision making about which collections to digitize and promote.

Good data can live forever. We have moved beyond wondering if the Machine Readable Cataloging standard is dead. It is alive and well and can be remixed and repurposed. The actual data is our product, not the online catalog. "Next-generation" discovery layers are using our bibliographic data in new ways to produce search results to next-generation users. Catalogers need to take an active role in the selection and customization of these products, as we know best where the data are and how data can be manipulated.

Metadata creators can move beyond the library and sell their services to academics and others with data organization needs. It is not as hard of a sell as one might think at first. Researchers are increasingly concerned with access to data sets, and access is difficult if not impossible if the data set lacks good metadata (Green 2009, 10). Library catalogers are practiced in standards creation and interpretation. There is much opportunity for catalogers/metadata creators to work with other information professionals and researchers to continually improve search tools and search results.

The sea change required in our community is reaction time and flexibility. We can no longer afford to take three years and three proposals to revise a single subfield code in a metadata standard. We need to rely on and trust one another and other academics to provide expertise. Catalogers, creators, and keepers of metadata have a tradition of embracing innovation. These innovations have historically remained behind the scenes. Now it is time to take that knowledge and innovation to the forefront of the digital library revolution. To do this, we need to build brand-name trust beyond our profession. We can build this trust by promoting the type of work we have excelled in for more than a century and engaging the twenty-first-century information seeker.

REFERENCES

Agourran, H. "Defining Information System Success in Germany." *International Journal of Information Management* 29, no. 2 (2009): 129–37.

Fontaine, M., and D. Millen. "Understanding Benefits and Impact of Communities of Practice." In *Knowledge Networks: Innovation through Communities of Practice* by P. Hildreth and C. Kimble. Hershey, PA: IGI Global, 2004. 1–13.

Green, T. "Published Data Needs Standards." *Research Information*, August/September 2009, 10.

Kimble, C. "Some Success Factors for the Communal Management of Knowledge." *International Journal of Information Management* 28, no. 6 (2008): 461–67.

Sancho-Thomas, P., and R. Fuentes-Fernandez. "Learning Teamwork Skills in University Programming Courses." *Computers & Education* 53 (2009): 517–31.

Viegener, T. "Switzerland Builds Next-Generation Metacatalogue." *Research Information*, August/September 2009, 18.

Index

About the Editor and Contributors

SEVER BORDEIANU is serials cataloging librarian at the University of New Mexico, where he has held many leadership positions in cataloging. He is currently a contributing editor for *Against the Grain*. He is also coauthor of *Outsourcing Library Operations in Academic Libraries: An Overview of Issues and Outcomes*.

ROBERT L. BOTHMANN, associate professor, is electronic access/catalog librarian at Minnesota State University, Mankato (MSU), where he serves as the cataloger for electronic and print monographs and journals and provides leadership and technical expertise for defining and providing access to electronic resources. He holds an MLIS from the University of Wisconsin–Milwaukee (December 2001) and an MS in geography and English technical communication from MSU (December 2005). He is the recipient of the 2007 Esther J. Piercy Award from the American Library Association's ALCTS division for outstanding contributions to librarianship in the field of technical services. He spends his spare time brushing up on German, playing with his dogs, kayaking, and camping.

KEVIN CLAIR is currently metadata librarian at the Pennsylvania State University Libraries, where he has worked since 2007. He holds a master of science in library science degree from the University of North Carolina at Chapel Hill.

ROBERT FREEBORN is the music/AV cataloging librarian at Pennsylvania State University. He has served on numerous committees for the Music Library Association (MLA), Music OCLC Users Group, and the Online Audiovisual Catalogers (OLAC). Currently, he is the chair of OLAC's Cataloging Policy Committee and a member of MLA's MARC Subcommittee of the Bibliographic Control Committee. He has also written numerous articles and given multiple talks on AV cataloging, heavy metal music librarianship, and cataloging organization.

AMY S. JACKSON is a digital initiatives librarian at the University of New Mexico, where she works with digital projects and the institutional repository. Prior to moving to New Mexico, she was the project coordinator for the IMLS-funded Digital Collections and Content project at the University of Illinois at Urbana–Champaign. She received her MLIS from Simmons College in Boston and also holds a master's degree in music from the Peabody Institute of the Johns Hopkins University.

DEBORAH LEE is the senior cataloger at the Courtauld Institute of Art book library, where her duties include cataloging training, authority control, and responsibility for the classification scheme. Previously, she held cataloging positions at the Natural History Museum and Oxford Union Society and worked as a research assistant for the AHRC Concert Programmes Project. She has a research interest in classification and has given a number of papers on the application of classification principles to performance ephemera in music. She was the 2008 winner of the IAML (Uk&Irl) E.T. Bryant prize.

REBECCA L. LUBAS is currently director of cataloging and discovery services at the University of New Mexico Libraries, where she coordinates a group of catalogers working in many formats. Before coming to New Mexico in 2008, she was at the Massachusetts Institute of Technology (MIT) Libraries as head of cataloging and metadata services and special formats cataloger. She was a founding member of MIT Libraries' Metadata Services Unit. Prior to her time at MIT, she was serials cataloger and audiovisual cataloger at Ball State University. She was president of the Online Audiovisual Catalogers in 2005 and a featured speaker at Library Week in Kosovo in 2006. She has an MA in English literature from Ball State University, an MLIS from Louisiana State University, and a BA from the University of Notre Dame.

BONNIE PARKS is the technology librarian and head of cataloging at the University of Portland in Portland, Oregon. She edits the "Serials Conversations" column for *Serials Review*. She enjoys teaching and frequently conducts training sessions for the Serials Cataloging Cooperative Training Program. She has taught graduate courses in information organization at Simmons College's Graduate School of Library and Information Science as well as at the University of Arizona's School of Information Resources and Library Science. Prior to assuming her position at the University of Portland, she was head of the serials cataloging section at the Massachusetts Institute of Technology.

JAY WEITZ is senior consulting database specialist at the Online Computer Library Center (OCLC). He serves as OCLC liaison to the Music OCLC Users Group, OnLine Audiovisual Catalogers, Music Library Association, American Library Association's Map and Geography Round Table, and PCC Standards Committee. He is also a member of IFLA's Cataloguing Committee and vice-chair of IFLA's Permanent UNIMARC Committee. He is the author of *Music Coding and Tagging* and *Cataloger's Judgment* and writes the cataloging question-and-answer columns of the *MOUG Newsletter* and the *OLAC Newsletter*. Since 1992, he has presented dozens of cataloging workshops in the United States, Canada, and Japan. He has a BA in English from the University of Pennsylvania, an MLS from Rutgers University, and an MA in education from Ohio State University. He was the recipient of the MOUG Distinguished Service Award in 2004 and OLAC's Nancy B. Olson Award in 2005.

GLEN WILEY is chief metadata librarian and head of metadata and batch processing services at Cornell University Library in Ithaca, New York. He leads a team of metadata, data, and database management experts responsible for providing consultation, design, production, and development services for the support of collections at Cornell and beyond. His interests are in technology, evolving metadata standards, and project management issues. He earned a BFA in the history of art and an MS in library and information science from Syracuse University.